'The remarkable story of how Wilma Johnson
reinvented herself – as she approached 50.'
The Mail on Sunday

'... tells house-bound housewives how it is possible to ditch
the dishes and sort out a life... Light-hearted yet hard-hitting.'
The Irish World

'... an exceptional memoir, *Surf Mama* is a tale to which
everyone can relate... Ultimately, an highly inspiring,
thoroughly enjoyable, and heartily recommended book.'
Plectrum – The Cultural Pick

'She casts a wry, often hilarious eye on her world, setting
the mundane against the bigger pictures of desire,
the past, existential possibilities, wine, espressos and
surf... She's a true artist and her book paints a bright
picture of surfing from an entirely different angle.'
Surfer's Path

'Johnson's account of her unlikely foray into the macho,
youth-driven world of wave riding... serves as a worthy
call to get out of the kitchen and into the water.'
www.24thletter.com

SURF MAMA

Summersdale Publishers Ltd
46 West Street
Chichester
West Sussex
PO19 1RP
UK

www.summersdale.com

Printed and bound by CPI Group (UK) Ltd, Croydon, CR0 4YY

ISBN: 978-1-84953-591-5

Substantial discounts on bulk quantities of Summersdale books are available to corporations, professional associations and other organisations. For details contact Nicky Douglas by telephone: +44 (0) 1243 756902, fax: +44 (0) 1243 786300 or email: nicky@summersdale.com.

SURF MAMA

ONE WOMAN'S SEARCH FOR LOVE, HAPPINESS AND THE PERFECT WAVE

Wilma Johnson

summersdale

For Daisy, Nat and Alice

CONTENTS

PROLOGUE

How would you like to stand like a god
before the crest of a monster billow?
Duke Kahanamoku

Do you ever get the feeling that you've walked on to the wrong movie set?

I was near Biarritz, on the Atlantic coast of France, in the Basque country. Biarritz has been a surf Mecca since the 1960s, when playboy millionaires would pull up on the Grande Plage in vintage Rolls-Royces full of longboards and pin-up beach babes. The scene around me was like a surfers' paradise. Big turquoise waves broke across the bay, exploding onto the reef and then disappearing into the blue lagoon in front of the Bahia beach bar, where the Beautiful People sipped rosé and ate foie gras. There were rainbows in the spray, which blew off the crests in the warm south wind; there were tanned demigods sashaying across the faces of the waves in flowery board shorts.

All was well on planet surf, but I wasn't quite sure what I was doing here. I could see that the waves were far too big for me when I got to the beach, but it was Sunday, and I like to keep Sunday special. I'd fed the kids and done some quadratic equations with them, in French. I'd done the barest minimum housework, because a friend had dropped by and asked me if I'd been burgled the week before. Now it was time for fun, and fun meant surfing. Of course there were lots of other things I could have done to relax on a Sunday afternoon: Biarritz is a town practically built for relaxing on Sunday afternoons. I could even have gone home and finished the housework. Perhaps it was that last thought that inspired me to pull on my wetsuit and paddle out into the set of *Big Wednesday*.

The trouble was that once I'd decided that I was going surfing, it was hard to give up on the idea. Someone had told me there were nice waves, which is like telling an alcoholic there's a nice bottle of malt whisky on the table next door. It wasn't just the need for the adrenalin rush of catching a wave, I felt as if I had to get off the land for a while, to see the world from a different angle. When you're out in the surf, your problems tend to dissolve into the foam. The next wave about to crash over your head seems a lot more important than the tragic state of your love life, your career or your bank balance. Or how to frame your latest masterpiece, or whether your 12-year-old daughter is too young to wear lip gloss or whatever else has been keeping you awake at night.

Looking back to the shore, I imagined other things I could have been doing. In the distance were the Art Deco casinos and hotels in Biarritz. I could have been playing roulette or drinking champagne with a wealthy lover in the Hôtel du Palais. I could have been eating oysters in the market or drinking hot chocolate in a Russian tea house. I could have been checking out the new lingerie collection in Galeries Lafayette. To the south the Basque coast stretched down to Spain, with the Pyrenees silhouetted behind. I could have been cruising down the corniche for a seaweed spa treatment in Hendaye, before crossing the border for tapas in San Sebastián. I could have been hiking in the hills, or following Ernest Hemingway's ghost round the bars and bullrings of Pamplona. So why was I out here waiting for these tidal waves to come rolling in and swallow me up?

I had to ask myself the age-old question: 'What the hell am I doing here?' Or, more precisely, 'What the hell am *I* doing here?'

For one thing I was the only woman in the water, which was not unusual. While the men go out like action heroes to prove themselves in the wild surf, women tend to stay on the beach doing sane and sensible things like sunbathing, reading or chatting with friends. Things that might sound like more fun than what I'm doing now, and I would have agreed until a couple of years ago when to everyone's surprise, including my own, I decided it was time to go out and join the boys.

At 44 I was pushing the recommended starting age by at least 30 years. General opinion is that two is a little early and 12 is a little late, but I've seen six-month-old babies surfing on their fathers' shoulders and dogs taking waves in the shore break. So, yes, 44 would have been a slow start even for a keen athlete, by which I mean someone who had ever seen the inside of a gym or done an exercise class. But if a tsunami did come in and my life flashed before my eyes, the great sporting moments would be few and far between. They might take up a split second or two in the highlights of my life, but no more. There would be studios and dripping paint, there'd be galleries, nightclubs and drinking clubs, love affairs and broken crockery. You might see me hitch-hiking round Iceland or Lapland in a long fur coat or strolling through Venice or Pompeii in a turban and platform shoes. You might see me wearing body paint or dancing salsa in a Mexican cantina. There'd be snatches of jungle and desert, pyramids and lava fields. Then there would be babies, green fields and windswept Irish beaches. But there wouldn't be much sport. I'm about as far as one could be from a classic surf chick.

I'm an artist. I was brought up in the London suburbs where women didn't surf, men didn't surf either and there wasn't even a wave machine in the local swimming pool. To me surfers were as exotic and other-worldly as Masai warriors, Inca queens or Mayan priestesses. They were on the other side of the world or in *National Geographic* or in *Hawaii Five-O* on a Saturday night.

I suppose that's why I'm so happy to be sitting here – even if my heart is pounding as though I've drunk a litre of espresso. I'm hypnotised watching the guys take off in what look like monster waves to me, but are probably just a bit of a laugh on a Sunday afternoon to them. I'm trying to sit far enough from the impact zone of the wave to avoid it breaking over me. Of course this means that I'm unlikely to catch anything, but that's OK by me. A few people pass and shout, 'You'll never get a wave there.'

'I know,' I smile back, 'that's the point.' They look confused and keep going.

But every now and then a set comes through. Waves are like London buses, you wait for ages, and then they all come at once – usually seven, in fact. It's not a good idea to take the first, because if you fall off it what happens next can feel a lot like getting run over by six buses.

I see a set come towards me. I could head for the horizon and escape it, but I've been out here long enough now to suspend my disbelief, to convince myself that I can do this, that I'm one of those exotic creatures who walk on water. The wave has to look like it's going to break on you for you to catch it, so you have to hold your nerve and not look back. I paddle down the face, and then I stand up as the board becomes weightless and starts to accelerate. I can hear the white water breaking behind me and see the glassy blue curve stretching out in front of me. The spray blows into my face, flickering with prisms in the sunlight. In a moment I might be under the wave swallowing seawater and small jellyfish, but right now I am an ancient princess of Hawaii, I am a bikini model, I am a goddess before the crest of a monster billow.

Part
One

THE WESTERNMOST BEACH BUNNY IN EUROPE

I was on a windswept beach on the Dingle Peninsula in Ireland when I had the revelation that I wanted to become a surfer. Here's how it happened.

It was the westernmost beach in Europe, just along from the westernmost bar, underneath the westernmost fisherman's cottage. I guess that made me the westernmost beach bunny in Europe, if you can be a beach bunny in oilskins. This is where St Brendan set out from in his cowhide canoe to discover America, a thousand years before Christopher Columbus or Amerigo Vespucci. He could have gone on an ego-trip and named the continent Brendania; New York would have been New Baile na nGall.

'Next parish Manhattan,' as Dingle locals like to say. It might be true that there's nothing but ocean between Slea Head and the Upper East Side, but they couldn't be more different, starting with the skyline. There are no skyscrapers here; instead of reaching up to scrape the sky, the buildings cling to the ground, keeping a low profile to avoid being blown away by Atlantic gales. Not that there are many buildings: the only signs of civilisation are a couple of old farmhouses, dry stone walls and a whitewashed crucifix on the cliff. It's too windy for trees: there are just rocks and emerald-green fields plunging into the sea, with a few sheep and clusters of wild arum lilies balanced precariously on their vertical slopes.

Further west are the Blasket Islands, uninhabited and deserted since 1953, with villages falling into ruins and the graveyards full of fishermen who drowned in the winter storms. Underwater cliffs shelve down to 50 metres, with wrecks of fishing boats and Spanish galleons in the abyss and Armada gold lost forever in the kelp forests.

Nearer the shore my husband, Nick, is surfing, alone except for a family of seals watching him as if they're trying to work out what strange sea mammal he could be. I'm on the beach making sandcastles and sandwiches, and doing a bit of low-maintenance yoga – trying not to fall asleep in Corpse pose in case the children drown in rock pools or come to blows over penny sweets. I get into a meditative mood, remembering how I ended up here in the very first place.

I first met Nick 12 years and three children ago in a drinking club in Soho. I was very intrigued when he told me he was a surfer; it seemed romantic and ethereal as if a blast of sea air had blown him into the smoky bar. I was struck by a sudden desire to learn to surf, images of following him out into the foamy brine flickered through my mind like ticker tape. Things looked promising when he invited me on a surf trip down to his home beach on the Welsh Riviera. But somewhere halfway down the M4 I began to sense that things were not going according to plan. There wasn't a palm tree in sight and it was sleeting heavily. By the time we got to Caswell Bay the sky was dark grey and the water looked like a windswept cappuccino. As I walked across the beach in a sleeveless wetsuit, it started to snow. Somehow I still imagined that when I dived through the foam, I would emerge in a tropical paradise. I dived. I emerged. I blinked twice waiting for a *Wizard of Oz* moment, but nothing had changed.

'Follow me outside,' he shouted. Which was weird, as I was sure I was outside already. After all, it *was* snowing.

Outside for a surfer is the place where the waves break in perfect tubes of shimmering turquoise water. Or in this case, the place where mountains of brown foam come crashing over your head to submerge you in a nightmare. I took one look at 'outside' and decided I didn't like it. I let the first wave sluice me onto the beach, and then ran back to the car where we'd left a bottle of whisky in the glove compartment for emergencies. I thought this counted.

Before I managed to recover from this traumatic experience and give it another try, I got pregnant. Everything is against the pregnant beginner: balancing with the bump, adding morning sickness to seasickness, the failure of wetsuit companies to provide a maternity range.

Six months after our daughter, Daisy, was born we moved to Ireland. On the face of it this seemed like a rather better place to learn to surf than London's East End, but if I thought the weather extreme and the waves hard core in Wales, then West Kerry had a few surprises in store.

The move was sudden and impulsive like a lot of our relationship: our first date was a fishing trip in North Carolina, our wedding six months later.

When Dr Johnson wrote: 'When a man is tired of London he is tired of life' he wasn't raising a baby in a housing co-op in Forest Gate. By the time Daisy was six months old I was *really* tired of London and especially tired of Platform 2a at Stratford Station and the nappy aisle of Sainsbury's. So when Nick suggested one Sunday morning that we should move to the west coast of Ireland, I didn't need much persuasion. We are both artists and it seemed like an exciting idea to escape from the big city art scene for a while. Property was incredibly cheap and we were able to put down a deposit on a four-bedroom farmhouse with the proceeds of our latest shows.

Then I read the Book That Changed My Life. The book that changes your life could be anything from the Bible to *The Dice Man* or *Quantum Physics for Dummies*: mine was *Three in a Bed*. Disappointingly it was a childcare manual, and nothing to do with *ménage à trois*. I already had a few How To Have A Baby manuals. The normal kind that explained, with illustrations, that at three months the foetus would be the size of a lima bean, at six months it would have eyelashes. By this time the mother would be wearing dungarees, have a hideous layered hair cut and a patient smile glued to her face. She would carry a giant straw basket of nappies wherever she went, just in case.

Three in a Bed was a bit different; it was based on Amazonian tribes and explained how children in the rainforest slept in their parents' hammocks and were breastfed until five years old. Apparently the kids grow up happy, well adjusted and intelligent. It must have been convincingly written, so for the next ten years I was either pregnant or breastfeeding. We ended up with three children, and if you do the maths that's five in a bed because the authors forgot the chapter on how to wean the kids and kick them out of the hammock. Or maybe they were too tired to write it.

Another chapter they omitted was the one on how Amazon mothers fared. The theory is great for the kids but not so good for parental sleep patterns, career or taking up water sports. Daisy, Nat and Alice may be happy, well adjusted and intelligent, but I'm not so sure about myself these days.

Perhaps I took the theory a bit far, I think as I sit on the beach, playing earth mother with home-made banana loaf and home-grown tomatoes in a picnic hamper. The children are running around me chattering away in Gaeilge (Irish Gaelic), looking like fairy folk with their wispy blonde hair and blue eyes while their father plays in the waves.

It's the classic man/woman, hunter/gatherer, surfer/beach bunny divide. I'm playing the role that woman has played since Time Immemorial: mother, nurturer, provider, Surf Widow. Changing nappies, feeding babies, collecting seaweed and mussels off the rocks for dinner. I'm happy with the stereotype right now, partly because what Nick is doing on a longboard seems so deeply and fundamentally scary, if not borderline psychotic. Every time I see another icy wave break over his head, I'm a little happier to be sitting on a beach blanket. I feel safer, warmer and drier. I dig my toes into the sand and cut another slice of banana loaf.

Recently, however, I've been feeling that it's not just women in general, but me personally who has been playing this role since Time Immemorial. I feel as if I've been sitting on the beach so long that I might turn into a rock formation or a monumental sculpture – the Madonna of Baile na nGall. It seems a long, long time ago when I thought I might surf; a long, long time ago that I came to Ireland for an adventure thinking I might stay a year or two.

I never imagined staying this long, but it's like the enchanted land of the west, whatever you choose to call it – Tir na nÓg, Atlantis, Brazil, fairyland or West Kerry. It's so beautiful that you fall under its spell and you don't notice time passing; then when you return home you wither and age and turn to dust.

But it's so hard to leave, just as it's hard to leave the bar on a Sunday night when the accordion music is playing and the old farmers are waltzing in their best suits. It's too easy to think you'll stay for one more pint and suddenly it's three in the morning. Or to think you'll stay for one more summer and suddenly you're 40. You have three children, a vegetable garden and some ducks. You also have a fine collection of nursing bras, but your paintings are gathering dust in an attic.

I think back to a night a couple of weeks earlier when it hit me that I might have been here longer than I intended. My friend Helena had asked me over to the next village to celebrate International Women's Day. I like celebrating International Women's Day as I've always seen myself as a bit of an International Woman, so I headed over to Ballyferriter for a pint. Halfway through the evening it occurred to me that Women's Day is usually in the spring, and it appeared to be mid-November. If you were feeling negative you could say that it always appears to be mid-November in Ballyferriter but...

'Oh, yes, but this is the International Day of the *Rural* Woman,' Helena told me.

What? This event sounded like something I might support by buying a packet of charity Christmas cards or a pair of hand-knitted alpaca bedsocks. I choked on my Guinness and started laughing. What did she mean 'rural woman'? I was born in London, I've lived in Paris and Mexico City, I'm a quarter Belgian – you don't get much more cosmopolitan than that. And even now though I live in Baile na nGall, a village with five houses and two pubs, it is 'next parish Manhattan' which must count for something.

'Are you OK?' she asked.

'Yes, it's just that I never really saw myself as a rural woman.'

'How long have you been in Baile na nGall?'

'Ten years.'

Now it was her turn to laugh. 'Well, if you weren't a rural woman when you arrived, you probably are by now!'

Should I get out the knitting needles and start on the bedsocks? Maybe they'd sell better than the paintings. I know that I'm Wilma, artist, traveller, adventurer, but to those around me I'm Daisy's mother who lives on the grassy road behind the Irish language radio station. It can be hard to continue believing your side of the story when everyone else believes something different.

The adventure has become reality. I'm no longer pretending to be a housewife in an Irish fishing village – I really am one. Or, if there is a difference, I'm the only one who can see it. I'm not an international art star or an international traveller after all; I'm an International Rural Woman.

At this very moment, picnicking on the windswept beach with my children and being a Rural Woman suits me fine because it means no one expects me to paddle out and take my chances in the swirling currents and icy waves. Thinking about it, it's unlikely that anyone ever expected me to surf – I've never seen a woman surfing in Ireland. And now that I'm over 40, no one will even expect me to try. For a moment it's a comforting thought.

Then I feel as if an icy wave *has* crashed over my head. What does this mean? That I will *never* learn to surf? That it's *too late*? That I'm *too old*? I realise that I've put my foot on the slippery slope towards knee rugs, bridge evenings and soft food. Alarm bells ring... I hear a little voice in my head saying, 'No, I can't be too old.' It gets a bit louder: 'NO, I can't accept this.' Then it turns into a banshee scream, drowning out the crashing waves, the gannets overhead and my kids complaining that they don't want seaweed for supper. 'NONONONONONO!' the voice shouts. 'I cannot be too old, I will become an extreme sports hero if I so choose.'

I'd like to say that I suddenly understood that the only thing to fear is fear itself and that I grabbed my husband's board, paddled out and took a monstrous wave, a school of wild dolphins by my side, my children cheering from the beach, while my slightly confused husband muttered 'What the feck?' under his breath and watched me with a new admiration.

But it didn't happen quite like that, and it would have made for a short book anyway. In fact I don't even mention my revelation to Nick because I know what would happen if I did. He would launch me in to the Blasket Sound in one of his old wetsuits. I would get washed around in the current, looking up at the whitewashed crucifix and wondering if a quick conversion would save me from my imminent doom. Then I would stagger up the beach shaking with cold and fear, covered in bruises and aching with chilblains, and he would say something really, really stupid like, 'Why didn't you take a wave?' And I'd say, 'Because I can't surf, obviously.'

So instead, I act as if nothing has happened. I keep quiet about my revelation because, although I've made the decision, there are a few small things standing in my way apart from the fear of fear itself. Such as the fact that I've never done any sport in my life, and that 12 years ago I already felt it was too late to start. This Amazon thing may be very good for the kids, but it doesn't exactly prepare one for extreme sports action. My training programme at the moment consists of soaking off my hangover in the Jacuzzi at the Skellig Hotel on a Sunday morning or walking up the lane with the pushchair to pick blackberries for a crumble. I appreciate that some physical preparation is required. I might start by getting out of the Jacuzzi from time to time and learning to swim front crawl. (Until I was 12 I swam on my back, but I got sick of banging my head on things so I taught myself breaststroke. Unfortunately neither of these strokes cuts it on a surfboard.)

So when Nick does come up the beach I say, 'Would you like seaweed for supper again, dude... I mean dear?'

I slip back smoothly into earth-mother mode. I pack up the picnic hamper and bundle the kids into their matching yellow oilskins, back at home I boil up the laver bread and feed the ducks. For a while everything continues as normal, but somewhere beneath the surface there's a surf chick waiting to hatch.

TIR NA NÓG

Oisín was one of the legendary warrior poets of ancient Ireland. He fell in love with a fairy princess and followed her over the sea to Tir na nÓg, the enchanted land of the west. After a while Oisín missed his friends and family, and asked the fairy princess if he could visit them. She let him go and gave him a white horse, but she warned him not to let his feet touch the ground. When he got home, he found that hundreds of years had passed without him noticing, and all the people he had known were dead. Oisín fell from his horse on Stradbally Strand, and when his feet touched the earth, he turned to dust.

I always wondered as a child why anyone would mind being trapped in fairyland; now I'm beginning to understand. I love this place, I love going to horse races on the beaches and swimming with wild dolphins, but I'm a London girl really, and Baile na nGall is a village of five houses. I used to get my dose of bright lights big city when I went over for exhibitions, but I've been going less and less recently and feeling more and more isolated. Also, being in the middle of nowhere isn't always the best thing for a relationship, as anyone who's seen *The Shining* will remember.

I receive a wake-up call a few weeks later when I go out to the US-style mailbox on the gatepost and find an invitation to a 20-year school reunion in Edgware. I look at it in disbelief. Although I think leaving school is something worth celebrating, I'm alarmed for two reasons. Firstly, how on earth did they find me in deep cover in the wilds of Baile na nGall? I feel like a war criminal who has been tracked down in the South American rainforest. Not enough plastic surgery, maybe.

Even more seriously than that, can I *really* be almost 40? Of course, I should know this, maths was my best subject at school and it's an easy sum. I've known since I was about three that my fortieth birthday would coincide with the millennium year. It seemed significant to me as a child. I'm sure Nostradamus has written an epic poem about the lead-up to my fortieth birthday and the apocalyptic events that will follow in its aftermath. I walk into the house in a daze and drop the letter on the kitchen table.

'Bad news?' Nick asks.

'Yes, I'm almost forty.'

'No you're not. I'm almost forty.' He's pulling rank. Technically I'm almost 39, but that's just like buying a dress that costs £39.99; you can pretend it cost thirty-something pounds, but you're not fooling anyone.

'It's all right for you – you don't have a biological clock.'

He laughs unsympathetically. 'You've got three children. Hasn't it stopped ticking yet?'

Maybe women's clocks don't always stop ticking. I met a woman in the swimming pool the other day who had 11 children. She tried to convince me that three was the hardest number and it got easier after that. I almost fell for it until she told me she was on her first weekend away from home for 20 years.

The invitation asks me to describe the past 20 years in fewer than 100 words. It's a classic mid-life crisis moment. What have I achieved? Have I let my dreams be dreams? Looking around me, I have to acknowledge I have an idyllic lifestyle: a whitewashed farmhouse with blue wooden shutters and honeysuckle growing over the porch, a garden full of roses, wild lilies and pampas grass. I've got three beautiful children; I've got poultry and a vegetable patch.

But suddenly I find myself wondering if this is what I wanted. I can't remember when I accepted the role of earth mother that I've spent so long playing – it was never on my list of life ambitions. I always saw myself as the sort of person who would run away with the circus or marry an Aztec warrior. Or become a surfer, a tanned queen of the waves, sculpted from pure muscle. I always imagined that by the time I was 40 I'd be a famous artist who had travelled the world, instead my paintings are growing cobwebs and my dreams of international jet-setting have been reduced to frequent-floater points on the Swansea–Cork ferry. I've never been to South America or Madagascar or Hong Kong; I've never even seen the water go down the plughole the wrong way.

It's as if Santa Claus got hold of the wrong Christmas list. What happened to my gallery in New York, my round-the-world air ticket and my Louis Vuitton luggage set? There's probably some woman halfway down the Pan-American Highway between Alaska and Tierra del Fuego wondering what happened to her poultry and her tomato plants.

'Are you going? I could look after the kids,' says Nick.

'Really? I could fly to Alaska, go down through California, Pacific coast of Mexico... ' I'm still lost in my fantasy world.

'What are you talking about? Are you going to the school reunion?'

Oh yes. Edgware. I could get the Northern line from Highgate and change at Camden Town. But do I want to?

School was not a pleasant experience for me: seven years of hell punctuated by weekends and holidays. I still have nightmares about it. I went to North London Collegiate School for Ladies (NLCS), which was founded as a forward-thinking girls' school in the nineteenth century, and hadn't changed in the intervening decades. We had to stand in assembly every morning and say prayers, which included things like: 'Let us pray for all those suffering in war and famine, and for the girls in upper fifth doing their needlework O-level.' and 'God give the hockey first eleven strength to prevail in their match against Haberdashers' Aske's this weekend.'

The school could never be accused of underestimating its importance in the grand scheme. Here's an excerpt from the school magazine, giving a brief history of the world according to NLCS:

1918: *Isabella Drummond arrives as Headmistress at NLCS. End of First World War.*

1919: *Uniform changed from blue to brown.*
Rutherford splits the atom.

I sometimes lie awake at night and wonder whether the atom would ever have been split if Isabella Drummond hadn't changed the colour of our uniform.

My years at NLCS were like walking into an old-fashioned schoolgirl novel by Angela Brazil or *The Chalet School Goes To Edgware*, except that my character was written by a different and altogether inappropriate author. I was in the wrong book. I said the wrong things. I wore the wrong clothes. I had the wrong pencil case. I didn't wear a vest and I couldn't knot my tie. I couldn't sing the hymns and I couldn't understand why on earth we weren't allowed to eat in school uniform, I'd always thought eating was a wholesome activity that grown-ups positively encouraged.

But worst of all I couldn't play netball. No one ever told me how. I just stood in the middle of the court wondering what the hell I was supposed to do while the Chalet girls yelled, 'Pass the ball, Johnson.' When they asked me what position I wanted to play I'd say 'floater'. That was the extra one who had no position; it was like volunteering to be the substitute. That's how I felt about school: I just wanted to sit on the bench, suck on an orange segment and wait until it was over. Without a doubt my best day of school was the day that I left. I threw my books onto the desk, walked out of the door and hitch-hiked to a Clash concert in Aylesbury for which Joe Strummer had put me on the guest list.

I first met my guitar hero in a bar in Camden Town a couple of months earlier.

'Hello, are you Joe Strummer? Do you want to buy me a drink?' I asked. It was a pretty lame chat-up line, and unusually forward considering I was pathologically shy at the time.

'I already have,' he said with the coolest smile in the history of rock and roll, and handed me a can of Colt 45. After that I bumped into him quite often at concerts and he always treated me to a few beers and put me on his guest list. Once he took me to lunch in a greasy spoon in Soho and afterwards bought me a piece of fabric in Berwick Street market. I was besotted and we made a date to meet the next day at a lunchtime rockabilly gig in Leicester Square, but I got stuck in a photography class and was very late. The gig had been cancelled and he had left. He went on tour and while he was gone I became a New Romantic, and due to the tribal nature of youth cults our paths never crossed again. I made the fabric into capri pants and wore them for years, and I've often cursed the cruel twist of fate whereby I was photographing pigeons in Charing Cross Road when I could have been on a date with my favourite rock star.

So the concert in Aylesbury seemed like a symbolic start to my Real Life, stretching out in front of me full of hitch-hiking, rock stars and American beer. I never saw anyone from school again, and I still can't wear brown pleated skirts or nylon gym knickers.

For a while I thought I *should* go to the reunion just to experience walking into my recurring nightmare. Would I stop having the nightmare if I went? Would I be able to show them that I was a glittering success of a person, despite their predictions of dismal failure? Or would I collapse in a crumpled

heap sobbing, 'Why didn't anyone tell me how to play netball?'
I sent a rather snotty description of My Life So Far to the
newsletter. It went something like this: 'After achieving a first-
class degree at the world-renowned Central Saint Martins
College of Art and Design, I have gone on to become an
internationally-acclaimed artist and have performed at the
Royal Opera House. I also have three incredibly beautiful and
talented children who can do long division in Irish.' So there.

No one needs to know that I haven't had a show in five years.
The sad truth is that I spend more time in the kitchen than
the studio these days, gutting salmon, inhumanely murdering
lobsters and baking banana loaf. But I'm getting my attack
in early. There was a real hothouse atmosphere at NLCS, so
I'm expecting to read a *Who's Who* of Nobel prize-winning
scientists, brain surgeons and netball champions.

But when the newsletter comes back no one else has boasted
about academic qualifications. It's full of heartfelt statements
like: 'Getting over a tricky divorce, sailing keeps me sane',
'Haven't done much since leaving, but I have some lovely cats'
and 'Wasn't school fun?'

So much for the hothouse flowers. Maybe my attack was a
little unnecessary? Maybe I should have given them my recipe
for banana loaf? I go inside and look in the mirror. Who is that
woman? She's wearing baggy salmon-pink tracksuit bottoms
and a large checked shirt over a 34F nursing bra, her hair is
a layered 1970s style without a hint of irony. At her age she
should know better than to go to a hairdresser who sports a
Rod Stewart hairdo. In short, I'm beginning to look like an
illustration in a childcare manual. If I sank into a bog right

now, archaeologists would dig me up in years to come and label me Millennium Housewife. 'We can accurately date her by the white Nike trainers.' I'd never get on a Clash guest list looking like this.

I'm not sure if I'm looking for an outfit that will convince the Old Girls that I'm rich, famous, successful and thin, or something that would tempt Joe Strummer to buy me a can of Colt 45, but I know I need help. My current look might be OK for the duck shed, but it won't get me on *The Kerryman* best-dressed list.

'Come on, Daisy, we're going shopping in Tralee.'

I reckon Daisy will make a good personal shopper. She's only eight, so her taste won't be middle-aged. I bundle all the kids into the back of the car promising them ice cream and red lemonade in return for styling tips.

Dingle is great if you're looking for an Aran jumper. It's also good if you're looking for Aran hats, socks, scarves or tea cosies. You can buy little Aran sheep reincarnated from their own wool, and I'm sure if you asked nicely they'd knit you up a nice Aran nursing bra.

I could try Foxy John Moriarty's, the pub where you can buy anything. It's like a game; you sit in the smoky front room with a glass of Guinness and try to think of something it might not have. I've bought a lot of things at Moriarty's: rat traps, fish hooks, chicken wire, coal, a double bed, bicycles, raspberry bushes, peat briquettes, a sou'wester. I think about walking in and asking for a new outfit and a pair of eyebrow tweezers, but it's a while since I got off the Dingle Peninsula, so I turn up over the Conor Pass and head for the bright lights of Tralee.

It's pouring. If the Inuk language has 50 different words for snow, the Irish language should have 60 for rain. There's soft rain and hard rain, driving rain and drizzle, there's good-for-the-complexion rain and the horizontal rain that comes in with the gales, torrential rain, sleet and hail, and then there's the Irish mist and the foggy dew. Today the winding road is scattered with dogfish, and for a while I think I've discovered a new kind of rain. It's easy to start believing things like dogfish rain when you've been on the peninsula too long. I'm kind of relieved when we catch up with a tractor full of fish, which are dropping onto the road.

The rain clears as we reach the top of the pass. There are no tourists, hikers or ambitious cyclists up here today, just some sheep that have been dipped and marked with dye that has run in the rain, so they're green, pink and blue. I look down towards Brandon Bay; the clouds float below us as if we're in a small plane.

'Look at that, kids, isn't it beautiful?'

'What? I'm bored,' says Nat, who is five. He's spent most of his life on the Dingle Peninsula and has probably had an overdose of dramatic landscape. He talks a lot about New York City, but I'm not sure if he believes it really exists.

'Darling, this is officially "one of the most beautiful places on earth". People come from all over the world to see this view.'

'Why?' he asks grumpily. 'It's only up the road.'

'Not if you live in Japan or America.'

Daisy looks at me sceptically. 'Yeah, Mum, like people come from "all over the world" to see... some rocks.' She rolls her eyes and she and Nat start laughing uncontrollably.

When we get down to town the Rose of Tralee is in full swing. It's a cross between a beauty pageant and a beer fest, all lip gloss and Guinness. The Roses are girls of Irish descent from all over the country and as far away as New York, New Zealand and Abu Dhabi, who descend on the town hoping to win the crown awarded for beauty, brains and quintessential Irishness. The betting shops, advertising 'Horses, Dogs, Politics', have dressed their windows with photos of the Roses smiling hopefully above the bookie's odds: Galway 10/1, Boston 25/1, Donegal 100/1. Why don't you just go home now, dear? I can see myself up there: Highgate 2000/1.

First stop is a place called Shindig. I park the pushchair in which Alice is sleeping peacefully, unaware of her mother's fashion-based existential crisis. She's only two and hasn't yet discovered the joy of shopping. I find myself gravitating towards the Guatemalan drawstring trousers and the hand-knit cardies.

'They're gross, Mum.' Daisy is right, I'm meant to be losing the childcare manual look. She hands me a lemon-yellow top with an eagle on the front and red fur sleeves. I look at the label: Custo Barcelona.

'Who the hell wears Custo Barcelona in Tralee?' I ask her.

'You do.'

You can't argue with your personal shopper, so I buy it and we move on to Young Scene (Daisy's choice). She picks out a glittery Lycra vest with 'slut' printed across the front.

'Mmmm.' I'm tempted, but would the Old Girls see the irony? 'Maybe a little *too* young for me, darling.'

'Not for you. For me.'

'What? Haven't you ever seen *Taxi Driver*?' Of course she hasn't. She's eight.

After an undignified fight we leave Young Scene empty-handed. As we walk across the square Daisy screams at me, 'You know nothing about fashion. You think you're the perfect mother, but all you know about is yoga and art!'

I buy some black trousers with lots of zips to go with the Custo top, and trainers with an 'anarchy' symbol moulded into the sole that will leave imprints in the sand. I must have been feeling nostalgic for my days as a Clash fan. After a few nightmares involving my old headmistress, Latin verbs and hockey sticks, I decide I don't really want to be reunited with that dismal era of my past. After all, I swore that afternoon when I hitched off to drink Colt 45 with Joe Strummer I would never set foot in the place again.

The Old Girls can use their imagination to fill in the gaps in my life story, and the strange new outfit goes down very well in the pub in Baile na nGall.

SEAWEED AND CHIPS

Maybe Daisy is right – maybe all I do know is yoga and art. I certainly haven't been transformed into queen of the surf, despite my revelation. As the winter closes in and the water temperature drops from chilly to arctic and the waves get wilder and more dangerous the surfing idea seems more like a moment of madness than a flash of inspiration. It doesn't put Nick off; he's surfed since he was 12 and his great-great-uncle was at the South Pole with Captain Scott. It's an unusually cold winter; he goes out in the snow and ice and climbs down cliff faces to reach the breaks. Afterwards he rings from the road to ask me to turn on the hot water and to go down to the pub to fetch a bottle of whiskey, and then he arrives home blue around the edges and shaking with cold. One day he comes in with blood dripping from a gash in his head and tells me his feet were so numb he slipped off the board and hit a rock. This doesn't really encourage me to join him.

I try to divert myself in other ways from making any major decisions about my life, such as whether I should leave Ireland. I know I've stayed much longer than I meant to, but it's hard to leave a place you love, so I convince myself that all I really need is a new hobby. I take Irish and karate evening classes, and I do a lot of yoga and art. I have a brief reincarnation as scuba woman. Then I start writing a Mexican cookbook based on a year I spent there before I was married, living in hotels and following the fiesta. Anyone with a bit of perspective could have told me that this wasn't a great way to get out of the kitchen.

They might also have told me that I was wishing I were somewhere else and feeling nostalgic for a time when I was less tied down; but I'm short on perspective and still haven't abandoned all hope of becoming Housewife of the Year.

I'm in the kitchen in immaculate make up and a tight cashmere jumper. I'm whipping up a passion fruit sorbet for the kids and dusting my chocolate brownies with a little gold leaf, expensive but worth the effort... Oh, no, that's not me. That's Nigella Lawson beaming down from the television in the corner of the cookbook shelf, somewhere between *Mexico: The Beautiful Cookbook* and *The Original Road Kill Cookbook*, telling me how to be a Domestic Goddess.

I'm more of a Domestic Antichrist tonight. I'm barefoot and covered in paint. I'm searching desperately through the freezer for some supper, but all I can find to go with the seaweed is half a bag of McCain oven chips.

'What exactly is wrong with seaweed and chips?' I ask the children irritably. 'Can't you be a little bit more... adventurous?'

Now Nigella's telling me it's 'really quite easy' to make ice cream while cooking your children breakfast and getting them off to school, and I'm willing to bet this woman has never microwaved a bowl of Ready brek chocolate porridge in the morning. At that moment there's a knock on the door. It's my next-door neighbour, one of the Baile na nGall salmon fishermen.

'We found these in the nets and we thought you might eat them.' He hands me two plastic carrier bags full of spider crabs.

We have a reputation locally for eating strange stuff. Since Nick started scuba diving he is summoned to clear propellers or search for anchors at dawn, and by way of thanks weird and wonderful creatures are left on the doorstep: a sunfish, a salmon with a seal-shaped bite out of it, crabs without claws, a lobster with a broken back. Suddenly all my feelings of inadequacy dissolve. I too can be a Domestic Goddess. Maybe not a cosy household one, more like Kali the goddess of destruction. I'm boiling a cauldron of salty water and telling the kids that spider crabs really wouldn't make good pets. Meanwhile the crabs have broken out of their plastic shopping bags and are littering the kitchen floor. A few have wandered into the garden and are crawling around in the rose beds making a surreal bid for freedom.

The water is boiling. 'No, kids, the spider crabs absolutely don't mind. They don't sit there at the bottom of the sea discussing art and philosophy, you know.'

Ten minutes later the crabs are piled up on a seafood platter with a little lemon. I've opened a bottle of wine and put on a Hawaiian shirt.

'Hey, Mum, this is amazing,' says Daisy picking up the hammer and smashing a claw. 'You should have your own TV show.'

I pour myself another glass of wine. Yes, I can see it...

'And for really special occasions I put a little gold leaf in the mayo.'

THE WICKER WOMAN

You may be wondering what I do with the seaweed. It might be tempting to imagine me in an exquisite kimono, like an oriental Nigella. I hate to spoil that charming image but this seaweed is laver, a Welsh delicacy that boils up into a greeny-brown pulp called laver bread, which goes well with bacon and cockles. It's been described by Richard Burton as 'Welshman's caviar', and by my children as 'looking like a cow pat'. But as I remind them every time I serve it up, it's full of iron and iodine and is sold at an exorbitant price in Harrods food hall to wealthy Welsh ex-pats.

'Then why don't you sell it to Harrods and use the money to buy us some real food?' the children ask.

'Real food' probably means exotic stuff like Big Macs and Happy Meals that they never get to taste because the nearest McDonald's is 240 kilometres away in Cork. It's the age-old fascination with the 'other'. My kids dream of junk food and shopping arcades, while children brought up in the city dream of windswept Irish wilderness and seaweed dinners... or maybe not.

My seaweed recipes went down better with the groups of surfers who passed through from time to time in search of the Perfect Wave. These were friends of my husband's from Wales, or friends of friends, along with a few total strangers and travelling surf stars. Sofa surfing was practically invented by surfers as a night time alternative to the usual kind, and if your sofa happens to be situated near a good break you risk having a pretty full house. But surf bums make good guests as they spend most of their waking life in the water or in the bar, don't mind sleeping in vans or cars if necessary and are also very appreciative of home-cooked salsa or seaweed. They were always men; it's a male-bonding thing, like deer hunting or golf. They were strange, sensitive creatures who could be thrown into deep depressions by small things like a shift in wind direction or a disappointing reading on an ocean buoy. I'd try to cheer them up with a plate of seaweed and chips and maybe some mussels or a spider crab if they were nice looking and they'd brought wine. Then they'd spend the evening discussing subjects of endless fascination to surfers and excruciating boredom to the rest of the world: offshore winds and underwater reefs, tidal coefficients and the consistency of different brands of board wax.

I would try to change the subject. Some came from New Zealand, South Africa or Australia, places I'd dreamed of visiting, but right now felt that I was destined only ever to see on the Discovery Channel. So I'd ask a leading question: 'What's it like where you come from, and does the water really go down the plughole the wrong way?'

What was I was expecting – a description of the flora and fauna, cultural highlights and local cuisine? I'm not sure, but what I got would be something more like: 'The river mouth works best on an incoming tide, but there are some mellow beach breaks as long as the wind stays south.' Which would start an hour-long discussion of ocean currents, trade winds and oceanic rock formations. I'd wander back into the kitchen to try and process the information while cooking up another vat of cockles and mussels. Previously I would have put their esoteric ramblings down to surf-induced psychosis and told my husband that his friends were about as interesting as an iceberg lettuce, but if I want to become a surfer I'll have to learn their language, which might be even harder than learning to swim front crawl.

But sometime that autumn I lose the will to be a Domestic Goddess and my kitchen starts to feel like the morgue of an aquarium. I find myself sneaking off to the pool and picking up a bag of frozen Donegal Catch on the way home. As I told the children, the *National Geographic* may have described this as 'one of the most beautiful places on earth' (and I'm sure they know their stuff), but suddenly all I can see is mud and sheep. My heart is not into earth-mother things anymore; I let the vegetable garden go to seed and my tomatoes wither on the vine. When a fox eats my ducks, I feel a sense of mild relief that I'm no longer the hen-woman of *Grimm's Fairy Tales*.

The winter depressions deepen; it's hard to say whether that's the shipping forecast or my psychologist's report. After two months of torrential rain the village looks like a giant mud bath and I understand why St Brendan set off to discover America, even though he risked falling off the edge of the world. I think most people in Baile na nGall would take that risk right now. Or maybe it's already happened? Maybe I've already fallen off the edge of the world? The visibility is about 3 metres, all I can see is the dry stone wall, a strip of barbed wire and a couple of miserable-looking sheep. The sheep are staring in through the window thinking more or less the same thing – mud and rain, mud and rain, what else is new? Same old stone wall, same old barbed wire, Wilma serving up another batch of spider crabs and another plate of seaweed. That woman needs to get a grip. Why doesn't she sell the seaweed to Harrods and buy a ticket to Honolulu?

Christmas, as you might expect, is a traditional affair round here, guilt and Guinness, 'Jingle Bells' and The Pogues' 'Fairytale of New York' blasting out from loudspeakers in Main Street, Father Christmas drinking in the village bar.

'Are you sure that was the real Father Christmas, Mum, 'cause he really smelled of beer?'

'It may have been one of his earthly representatives, darling.'

And then there's the usual argument with the school about whether or not Daisy will be singing in the angelic chorus at midnight Mass. She's not Catholic, I explain for the hundredth time, so she will not be at Mass and she won't be taking confession either. She'll just have to live with the guilt of having coveted her friend's Butterfly Princess Barbie for another year. The staff give me a look reserved for pagan earth mothers willing to send their innocent children to the fiery gates of hell on a whim, and give me the address of the nearest Protestant church. They don't know that I've only been to church once in my life, and that was when I was a Girl Guide and I had a crush on the Chaffinch patrol leader.

Daisy did have a brief flirtation with religion.

'Mum, I think you should become Catholic,' she told me one evening.

I'm worried for a moment. Baile na nGall is exactly the sort of place where young girls have visions of Holy Virgins on hillsides.

'Why aren't we Catholic anyway?'

'I just wasn't born that way, honey.' I do have some Methodist missionaries somewhere in the family tree, but not too close for comfort.

'Well, thanks, Mum, because every other girl in the class gets a white wedding dress and £200 from their uncles and aunts when they do Communion. I get nothing at all, so you might want to think about becoming a Catholic.'

'I don't think that would work in our family, darling.'

At least she hasn't had a vision. I ask Auntie Lizzy to send over some Buddhist prayer beads, and I give Daisy £10 and buy her a new dress and a pair of platform shoes as a compromise.

On 26 December, Dingle reverts to good old-fashioned pagan values with the carnival atmosphere of Wren's Day. The wren was a sacred bird to the Druids who predicted the future by its flight path. Church leaders later put their own spin on it, but Wren's Day has kept the flavour of a pagan festival, an antidote to Christmas, which is the only day of the year when the bars close. Today, the 52 bars in Dingle open at dawn and the sound of high-pitched tin whistles and the ominous beat of the bodhrán drum fill the air. The lanes are full of people dressed top to toe in suits woven from straw, and capes, skirts and cone-shaped hoods topped with horns. The moving haystacks can seem quite sinister.

Other characters in the ritual are a wooden hobby horse that whirls around knocking over anything in its path, a mysterious 'man from the East' and an old washerwoman. No one has ever explained what any of it means; maybe I'm too much of an outsider, or maybe it's been lost in the mists of time and Guinness.

Other people dress in masks, rubbish sacks and whatever comes to hand. I toy with the idea of wearing a grass hula skirt Alice got for Christmas but a hailstorm puts me off. I settle for a couple of feathered Mexican masks and go to Dingle to meet my friend Kate, a Kerry girl who now lives in Dublin. Kate and I have spent whole summers sitting on Baile na nGall Beach and she's the one of the people I'll miss most if I leave.

The Dingle Wren is probably the only time you'll see Baile na nGall fishermen wearing dresses, but you'll never know for sure because the disguises are impenetrable. The men wear rubber gloves so you won't recognise their hands and talk in trilling soprano voices so you have no idea who they are. You never refuse to buy a drink for anyone on Wren's Day, especially not if you're English.

One of the wicker men comes up, takes me by the waist and swirls me around to dance to the beat of the bodhrán drum.

He might be one of the salmon fishermen, he might be my karate teacher, he might be the ghost of a Druid who has come to Dingle specifically to tell me I've baked enough banana loaf and it's time to get on with my life. 'You don't know who I am, Wilma, but I know who you are,' he says in a high-pitched banshee voice, full of pagan wisdom.

You do? So who am I? Am I Rural Woman or Bond Girl? The hobby horse snaps its wooden teeth, the band strikes up again and my oracle moves up Green Street to the next bar. Damn, what colour gloves was he wearing?

'Are you OK?' Kate asks me, feathers blowing off her Mardi Gras mask.

'I don't know. Which way are the wrens flying?'

'The wrens have been swept over Mount Brandon by the hurricane. Which means, as far as I know, that we should head down to Moriarty's for another pint.'

In the bar, the old men sing and the whistles play tunes of famine, love and rebellion and the distant shores of countries for which you leave knowing you'll never return.

'How are you anyway?' Kate asks me.

It might be the smoky atmosphere in the bar, the icy cold wind or feathers from my mask in my eyes, but my eyes fill with tears.

'I don't know, I think I need to get out of here.'

'Do you want to move up to Dick Mack's?'

'No, I mean really get out of here, leave Ireland.'

'You've been here a long time, maybe it *is* time to go.'

I'm beginning to realise that karate and yoga and exotic recipes aren't enough. I can discover my inner samurai, stand on my head and cook iguanas all I like, but really they are all just a distraction from making the decision to leave.

THE BURNING BUSH

I decide to clear out the studio the next day, and I light a bonfire at the end of the garden to burn the rubbish. It's a symbolic cleansing process, death of the old year, birth of the new. Wren's Day has gone to my head. Or perhaps I'm slowly preparing to leave. I start with old drawings, the kids' old homework and broken pencils. A few Pokémon cards get caught up in the trash.

'Oh no, Mum, I can't believe you just burned Venusaur, it's the evolved state of Bulbasaur, it's got one hundred and seventy-nine attack points and it's very, very rare,' moans Nat.

I'm not in the mood for a guilt trip; I'm developing a mild case of pyromania.

I move on to the clothes: sheepskin slippers in which mice have nested, my apron, tracksuit trousers, nursing bras. The Christmas tree: it looks a bit dry, and never mind if there are still a few decorations on it, I'm getting into my winter solstice ritual, it's Saturnalia, death and rebirth of the sun...

'Mum, you just burned Father Christmas!' wails Daisy.

As I said, I'm not accepting a guilt trip. I'm reclaiming Santa Claus as a pagan god form. A Norse deity invented by the Sami people of Lapland when they were hallucinating Santa Claus and his flying reindeer after eating red and white fly agaric toadstools. Santa is, in fact, the human embodiment of a fly agaric. I'm not sure how much of this ancient wisdom I should share with Daisy and Nat.

'Father Christmas is a toadstool.'

'Oh, God, Mum's finally lost it. Let's go and watch Cartoon Network, Nat.'

Just as they get into the house, the Christmas tree topples off the fire and ignites the old, plastic roof box from the car. The box explodes in a plume of smoke 20 metres high and covers the village in an evil-smelling black cloud. When it clears a fine black rain of fragments of my past is falling over Baile na nGall. I'm standing in the middle of it in my oranges and lemons dressing gown and wellingtons, flecks of ash on my face and in my hair, a bucket of water in one hand. Even the cows are staring at me as though I'm crazy.

One of the fishermen walks past.

'*Conas atá tú?*' How are you?

'*Go-maith.*' I'm fine.

He nods politely and walks on down to the pub, leaving me staring at the smoldering hedge.

In the middle of the hedge is a flaming blackthorn bush screaming at me, 'I am a burning bush. I am a sign. What more do you need, you stupid woman, how much more bloody obvious can I make it? It is time to change your life.'

Maybe it's time to start paying attention to the signs – if they get any more dramatic I could be in real trouble!

Part Two

THE BEAUTIFUL PEOPLE

I can't take the decision alone, but my husband is ready for a change too – we're beginning to feel that things aren't working in Ireland. We know it's not just the location, and we both hope that things might improve between us if we move.

There is a theory that you can't escape your problems by taking them to an exotic location. But if you are going to split up, at least you will have some good photos and a suntan as a consolation.

It takes a while to decide where to move. We take trips round the coast of Europe in our rusty old camper van, combining exhibitions in London, Paris and Milan with the search for a new place to live: the destination and the length of the trip depending on weather forecasts and how many paintings we've sold. The essential features we're looking for in our new home are good schools and bars and west-facing beaches for surfable waves – my husband insists on this, but obviously it suits my secret mission. It also has to be within striking distance of London for shows or have a good art scene (although the beach clause pretty much counts that out).

The trips vacillate between hippy dream and hippy nightmare.

Sometimes it feels like there are endless possibilities for the journey and for our relationship. As we drive across Spanish sierras, through Portuguese cork forests and meadows full of flowers, and camp on deserted Atlantic beaches lulled to sleep by the sound of surf and cicadas, we feel that it's all going to work out, we just needed to get out of Baile na nGall. We could head south to Morocco and on to Timbuktu. We could settle down in a fishing port and live on fresh sardines from the market and Sagres beer.

But it's a fragile balance – if it rains for more than a day or the van breaks down, the mood shifts and the sense of optimism quickly dissolves. Most of you have probably been on a long drive arguing with your partner or been stuck in a car with a bunch of screaming children, counting the minutes until you reach your destination. Now combine the two experiences and imagine that the journey has no end, and you're sleeping and cooking in your car.

Trying to keep five people amused in a space 2 metres square isn't easy – especially when three of them are too young to sample the local rosé.

I'm not completely sure whether we chose Biarritz because the French school system is so good or because it picks up the best of the Atlantic swell; let's say there was something for everyone. We certainly didn't choose it for the art scene. Although Picasso spent his first honeymoon there and a lot of artists have been attracted to the area by the southern light and bohemian lifestyle, the galleries show a depressing mixture of kitsch touristy themes: dead bulls and men in tights, fishing boats and men in berets, sunset over the ocean and even crying clowns.

We move to a village just south of Biarritz called Olatua, selling the farmhouse to buy an apartment in a beautiful Art Deco building that used to be a hotel and casino in the 1930s. The old women in the village reminisce about dancing in the roof garden, the old men about gambling in the basement. We have two balconies that look out over the surf spot with the biggest waves on the coast.

We arrive fresh from the wild west of Ireland in oilskins and wellingtons and find ourselves plunged into the world of the Beautiful People – it's not that they are literally more beautiful than people in Ireland, it's just that they look as if they've spent a few hours with a stylist before leaving the house. It might sound fun to be plunged into the world of the Beautiful People – and I'm sure it would be if you were invisible – but there's pressure. In Olatua the road sweepers look like models and even the local tramp has blond streaks put in for the summer. Department 64 (officially Pyrénées-Atlantiques, unofficially Pays Basque) is so chic it has a clothing brand named after it. You have to check your lipstick before you go out for a baguette in the morning, and on the way to the shop you'll have to kiss six people – friends, acquaintances and complete strangers – while simultaneously delivering an accurate surf report.

Kiss kiss, 'Two to three metres and glassy.' Other cheek, kiss kiss, 'Offshore wind, but it might change at low tide. That's two forty-five in the afternoon. *Bonne journée*!'

The language is a culture shock, but it's nothing compared to the beach. A nursing bra definitely does not count as swimwear. The sand is littered with the bodies of semi-naked film stars and supermodels stretched out in the sun like victims of a self-inflicted famine. You could shoot the *Sports Illustrated* swimsuit issue without hiring models.

Fat as a feminist issue isn't a concept that holds much sway in France. French women do eat foie gras; I've seen them do it. I've seen them fry it, put it on toast and pop it in their mouths. The mystery is what happens to it next; it simply disappears without trace. I've checked their ankles, thinking maybe it sinks, but no. No sign of it anywhere. Maybe they have really, really fat livers, but you can get away with that in a bikini. French women may have only got the vote in 1944, but I suspect there was a subclause in the legislation stipulating that they would never wear plain cotton underwear or drink beer from a pint glass in exchange for their emancipation.

I buy a lip gloss one day, and the whole thing is explained to me in a nutshell on the packaging. In French, the lip gloss promises 'irresistible seduction'. In the English text, this is 'translated' as 'long-lasting comfort'. That's the difference between French and English women. We love our Marks & Spencer five-pack, 100-per-cent cotton briefs. Long-lasting comfort. I'm sure even the frumpiest French women wear insanely sexy underwear. I've seen old ladies in Biarritz dressed in nylon tent dresses buying red lace thongs. Irresistible seduction.

Sometimes I miss the days when I could go down to Baile na nGall beach with my oilskins over my bikini and meet my friends for a pint. And in Baile na nGall we understood the meaning of the word relaxation. We'd sit under the wall watching the kids making sandcastles, then someone would get out a mobile phone, call TP's bar and ask them to pass a couple of pints of cider over the wall. We weren't really too lazy to walk up the steps, but it involved getting dressed and that seemed a bit like hard work. But on Olatua *plage* everyone's surfing, running, doing gymnastic displays or paddling Hawaiian-style canoes back and forth on the horizon. It's exhausting just watching.

If fat is not a feminist issue, body hair is completely taboo. Even during the height of the terrorism threat, Biarritz airport never banned eyebrow tweezers in cabin luggage. Proof that the French are more scared of women with body hair than terrorists.

I've always felt that life was too short to waste it in a beauty parlour, and I've arrived from a place where the weather was too cold to dispense with any natural body defences. But now I suspect I have more armpit hair than any woman in Department 64, possibly more armpit hair than all the women in 64 put together. This is brought home to me one day on the beach when a male surfer comes up and says, 'Wow, armpit hair, cool. You remind me of my girlfriends in Hawaii in the 1970s who drank beer and didn't shave!' I get the impression that he hasn't seen a woman with unshaved armpits for 30 years, and sees me as a museum piece or the spearhead of a hippy revival. For a while I resist the pressure to conform – shave your armpits and you open the door to a return to patriarchal dictatorship – but the kids aren't so impressed by the vintage look and tell me I can't be the only woman on the beach who looks as if she has hamsters nesting under her arms.

If they have to learn the language, I have to accept the culture. I reluctantly buy a Venus Gillette razor wondering if the 1970s ever happened.

It was probably naive to think that I'd avoid the pressure by going to the naturist beach. I'd fondly imagined that the designer swimsuit and the Brazilian wax would be redundant. No bikini, no bikini line, surely? I drag the kids along, with a bit of opposition.

'What's the matter with you? Do you actually *like* looking at naked people?' Nat asks in his best 'disgusted of Tunbridge Wells' voice.

'The human body is a beautiful thing.' I hold my tummy in as I say it.

'Oh no, Daisy, this is awful. Our mother's a pervert.'

That's the trouble with the younger generation, you try to teach them good, old-fashioned hippy values like free love, carrot cake and nude sunbathing, and they turn all puritanical on you. But when I get to the beach it hits me that without clothes there is nothing left but grooming. Grooming and accessories: gold jewellery, designer sunglasses and designer dogs. The first thing I see is a woman taking a pair of tweezers out of her Prada handbag to perfect her Brazilian wax, which seems to be taking grooming to psychotic extremes.

You have to get your head round the beach etiquette because the beach is the social centre of the village along with the terrace above it, which looks out over the wave. Under the terrace is the village bar. This canteen of the Beautiful People is so not the traditional French village bar of *A Year in Provence*. There's a mixture of Senegalese kitsch, Hindu shrines, lace curtains and plastic Mexican tablecloths. Vintage surfboards and African plastic buckets hang from the ceiling; a hand-written sign behind the bar reads: 'Jah Rules – everything comes in its own time.' This includes the drinks – beer, sangria or killer rum punch – but be grateful for the wait because you won't get served at all if you don't have the right karma. The owner Patrique is a style icon to the masses; sometimes I go down when I'm not even thirsty just to check out his shirt: antique silk ruffles, African batik or vintage aloha. His glamorous Spanish wife will be played by Penelope Cruz in the movie. You could really meet anyone in the world in this bar: surf legends and footballers, Parisian philosophers, movie stars, squid fishermen, photographers and firemen. Or you could meet no one at all – the atmosphere and the clientele change completely with the direction of the wind.

The same is true of the rest of the village. If the swell is big and the wind is offshore the sky will be blue, the air will taste of salt and adrenalin and there will be rainbows in the spray blowing off the back of the waves. The terrace will be thronging with spectators and film crews watching the surfers, some kid with dreadlocks will get overexcited and start playing the bongo drums, and the bars will be full of bikini models and sexy men in flip-flops. If it's onshore and flat, it's probably raining and you'll be lucky to see an old couple walking their poodle. The bars will be closed, with the shutters down, as if you couldn't drink beer in the rain.

Olatua is dominated by the wave. Sometimes the ocean is dead calm, sometimes the waves are small, crowded with kids, longboarders and tandem surfers holding petite women above their heads on outstretched arms. Sometimes it's an ugly grey mess and there's nothing out there but seagulls, a dead dog and Spanish rubbish sweeping in from the super-dump in La Coruña. And sometimes it's like Hawaii. Everyone surfs. At least that's what I think at first watching kids and 70-year-old men paddle out, dogs being pushed into waves and babies being initiated into the ocean before they can walk. It takes me a while to notice that in this great multi-generational surf fest there are practically no women. I do finally see one woman paddle out and then I think I see another a week or two later, but eventually it clicks that it's always the same woman! One day I see a group of girls out there and get quite excited until I look closer and see that they're men with dreadlocks.

I never saw any women surfing in Ireland either, but there weren't many surfers so it was less surprising. Maybe the absence of female surfers should put me off, but it just makes me more determined. I've got to get in the water.

UNDERSTANDING CAMUS

Having studied it for ten years at school, I'm surprised to discover after the move that I don't speak French. I hadn't anticipated much of a problem because, while I was studying for my A-level, I was under the impression that I was making profound analyses of existentialist literature. But now I find that I'm scarcely able to order a cup of coffee. Perhaps it was Mme Gillespie who was doing the detailed analysis all along, and I was simply copying it off the blackboard while wearing a black polo neck and matching lipstick.

In my defence it's not so easy to order a cup of coffee in France due to the legendary snootiness of French waiters. There may be some parts of the country where baristas have less attitude than in Paris, and simply say, 'Coffee, of course, milk, sugar, marshmallow topping?' But Biarritz is on a par with the Champs-Élysées except that instead of wearing those silly old-fashioned aprons, they'll be wearing board shorts, designer flip-flops and not much else. Who do I have to sleep with to get a coffee round here? Not that I'd mind if I thought I stood a chance, but the waitresses have a tendency to look like Brazilian movie stars, so the waiters are probably doing OK without me.

My children may never forgive me for putting them into the local school when their only words of French were *bonjour, au revoir* and *croissant*. I did try to teach them before resorting to the immersion technique. We would sit in the car with a language cassette playing, me hoping that they would pick up the basics on the way to the supermarket. '*Un, deux, trois...* '

'Come on kids: *un, deux, trois, quatre, cinq...* ' I'm trying to sound cheerful, but I still haven't recovered from the fact that I never really understood Camus after all.

'*A haon, a dó, a trí, a ceathair, a cúig...* '

'Daisy, that's Irish, you know it is.'

'You never learned Irish. Why should I learn French?'

'Because we live in France now, honey.'

'And whose fault is that? You sold our house in the most beautiful place on earth and brought us to live in a country where you can't even order a glass of wine.'

It would be fair to say that at this point Daisy isn't entirely happy with the move.

'Come on, you'll thank me when you're bilingual.'

'I'm bilingual already, thanks. I speak Irish.'

This is true. While Daisy was representing Murriegh Junior School on Radio na Gaeltacht, the only phrases I had mastered after ten years were *póg mo thón* (kiss my arse) and *dún an doras* (shut the door). Don't ask me why, those are just the first things you learn.

'Well, trilingual, even better. You'll see, you'll pick it up in no time.'

'Really? How come you learned it for ten years at school and you can't speak it yet?'

'Because, for your information, I was too busy studying existentialist literature to bother with mundane stuff like that. Would you like a *pain au chocolat* when we get to the supermarket?'

'No, I want some home-made lemon meringue pie from Baile na nGall post office. But I can't have it, can I? Because you sold our house in the most beautiful...'

School starts on Monday, and if the immersion technique doesn't work at least it will get them out of the house and give me a few hours' break from the 24-hour guilt trip. The kids come out of the *école primaire* on the first day looking a little pale.

'Thanks, Mum,' Nat says. 'That was the worst day of my entire life.' And then he doesn't say another word to me for two days.

We walk back to the apartment with Daisy muttering under her breath, 'I can't wait to put this in my memoirs, and then people will know what you're *really* like.'

Daisy shows me her homework – a surrealist poem three-pages long to memorise and a list of about a hundred words to learn for a dictation test tomorrow. 'Oh and these verbs in these tenses,' she adds handing me the list: *imparfait, passé simple, futur, plus-que-parfait, passé antérieur*. What the hell are these?

I'm pretty sure I explained to her teacher that she only spoke three words of French – he's taking the immersion technique pretty seriously.

'So what's the poem about?' asks Daisy.

Rivière and *coucher du soleil* are the only words I recognise. What did they teach us at school?

'It's something about a river at sunset,' I say, struggling to sound confident.

'There must be more to it than that, there's three pages. What did they teach you at school?' Daisy isn't impressed.

'Oh, I don't know. In Albert Camus's masterpiece of existentialist literature, *La Peste* is not just the plague, it's a metaphor for the Nazi occupation of France and the way people's minds and souls can be poisoned by propaganda and fear.'

'What?'

'Never mind, let's go to the supermarket and buy a dictionary.'

But the immersion technique works and after a few months they're chattering away in French. Within a few more months they're correcting my grammar, and by the end of a year they're taking the piss out of my accent and suggesting I should take a French evening class. Or a French lover.

TOTAL ECLIPSE
OF THE BRAIN

I initially arrived in Biarritz with my husband. We made the common mistake of thinking our relationship would improve if we moved to a place with lots of sunshine and cheap alcohol. Two years later I was suntanned and hungover, but things hadn't miraculously improved. One day I heard myself arguing with him and thought, Oh God, if I don't leave soon, I'm not going to give myself an ulcer, I'm going to turn into one.

Is turning into an ulcer grounds for divorce? I don't know.

I could write a whole book about splitting up, but let's face it, other peoples' marital break-ups are totally boring to the rest of the world unless the couple involved are high-profile millionaires over whose predicament we can gloat.

We all like to think we're unique, especially in our darkest hours. But the other day I was watching daytime TV and found myself wondering if the scriptwriters for this divorce sitcom had planted a CCTV camera in our apartment. You might go to hell and back and plunge into the ugly depths of your subconscious, but after all that your arguments end up packed with playground lines like 'I can draw better than you!' and 'Aren't you a bit old to wear a belly top?'

So here's a more concise version – I knew it was over so I told Nick I was leaving. What I meant was that I was leaving the relationship, and I'd like him to leave the flat.

His response was: if I was leaving I could leave, but he wasn't going anywhere.

I guess I should have seen that coming.

After a four-month stand off with me sleeping on the sofa I accepted that I was either going to lose my sea view or lose my mind. I took my half of the deposit on the apartment and rented an elegant but dilapidated house on the other side of the village. In the eyes of the world – or let's say Olatua, which has become my world – I'm a bit of a bitch for leaving, and I've added insult to injury by *not* leaving him for a Frenchman. That would have been understandable. *L'amour fou* is a very French concept of insane, obsessional love that tips you into a vortex of desire. It was a central theme of surrealist philosophy, giving it an extra edge – you imagine *amour fou* only happens between very beautiful but slightly deranged people dressed in cocktail gowns and tuxedos, or not at all. It's a pardonable offence; people will say, 'Oh she was wrong to leave but,' lowering their voices to an awed whisper, 'it was *l'amour fou*, you know.' It's like a force of nature, an act of God and you can't insure yourself against it.

Being in the same village as Nick is convenient for the kids, but awkward for us. We flip a coin every weekend to decide who's allowed to go to the bar so we don't bump into each other. He gets heads and tails; I can only win if the coin lands on its edge, because after all I was the one who left. I understand it is going to be impossible to avoid my ex in a village this size, but I feel like someone is taking the piss when I drive the kids to school one morning and see the men from the town hall erecting a huge banner over the main road bearing Nick's name.

Nick has a one-man show of his paintings in the local museum, and every shop, bar and restaurant has a poster in the window. As if that wasn't enough, one of the surf companies has put out a special 'artist's collection' of beachwear to coincide with the show, so women are walking around the village wearing sundresses, T-shirts and flip-flops printed with his paintings, and the beach is covered with glamorous women in his bikinis lying on his limited-edition beach towels.

I finally leave the apartment on the eve of a solar eclipse – I hadn't planned the Nostradamus touch, but I suppose it added an element of drama, if it needed one – and the children and I move into the magnificent but dilapidated *belle époque* villa, known to the local children as 'the haunted house'. The house is pink with green shutters and ivy grows up the walls inside and out.

After the emotion of walking out after 15 years I hadn't really thought through the practicalities of the situation. As the kids and I prepare to spend our first night in the house, I realise that apart from leaving my husband I have also left my cooker and most of my furniture. All I've brought are a few mattresses and the TV that a friend gave me.

It's a dark and stormy night, the shutters are creaking, the attic doors are slamming, the light bulbs flicker and occasionally explode. There are barn owls and screech owls and bats in the garden, my hound howls like a werewolf at full moon and the kitten wanders around all night crying 'Mamaaaa, Mamaaa' like a demented changeling. The *Hammer House of Horror* sound effects get on my nerves, so I go to put on some cheery music – but of course I've left the stereo behind with just about everything else.

'Anyone fancy a takeaway Happy Meal?' (The fridge wouldn't fit in the car.)

We sit on the floor eating McDonald's and watching a TV show called *On a échangé nos mamans*, where two families swap mothers for a week. My kids are looking as if they'd take, more or less, any other mum on offer.

'That pig farmer from Alsace was quite sweet underneath it all, wasn't she?'

'I liked the lighthouse keeper's wife. Her house looked cosy.'

Thank God they serve beer in McDonald's here.

The next day is the eclipse and I've volunteered to go on Alice's school trip to the Château d'Abbadie, down the coast near Hendaye. The chateau was built by Antoine d'Abbadie, an eccentric Irish/Basque aristocrat who took inspiration from his Celtic heritage and his travels through Ethiopia. The result is a surreal mix: a neo-Gothic castle built on the cliff top; elephants, crocodiles and monkeys carved into the stonework; and *Céad Míle Fáilte* – 'a hundred thousand welcomes' in Irish – written above the door. I love the castle, but I am slightly disappointed by the nature of the welcome.

I was imagining being greeted by some elegant and aristocratic descendant of Monsieur d'Abbadie, a little foie gras and champagne brought out by maids in starched uniforms. Maybe a touch of *l'amour fou*, in this appropriately surreal setting. Disappointingly the chateau was donated to scientific research years ago, so the garden is full of serious-looking astronomers. None of them seem interested in being swept into a vortex of desire with me.

I'm supposed to explain to a class of nine year olds exactly how an eclipse happens. In French.

'Is it the shadow of the earth on the sun, or the moon on the earth?' I whisper to my friend Florence. I haven't slept much and I'm getting confused, and to make matters worse Bonnie Tyler is singing 'Total Eclipse of the Heart' on a loop tape in my head. Like Bonnie, I have the distinct impression that I'm falling apart, mentally and physically.

The stupid thing about going to see an eclipse is that you're not allowed to look at it. The kids are wearing dark eye masks that cut vision to almost zero, they are looking down tracing the shadows of shadows cast on to tabletops, tripping over and bumping into each other. Meanwhile I'm explaining that the eclipse is the shadow of the moon crossing the sun or something to do with Bonnie Tyler's love life.

In the end I leave the science to the scientists and sneak into the house. It's full of tartan and red velvet, ebony panels carved with mysterious messages in ancient African languages. The light of the eclipsing sun slants through the windows onto antelope and stag heads hanging on the walls. I start to feel completely spaced out and wonder whether I'm actually dreaming the whole thing. By the time the children get back from school, I'm pretty much seeing double from exhaustion.

I've been a single mother for less than 24 hours and I need a break already. They're a little confused by the situation in general, and more particularly why I've brought them to live in a house with no hot food and no beds when their dad is just down the road with wall-to-wall carpet and a shelf full of Japanese cookbooks.

'Now what does this house *need*?' I ask in the most cheerful mumsy voice I can conjure, spraying Freshly Baked Scone room perfume around the place.

'Beds, carpets, a cooker, curtains, cupboards, lights, more TVs, heating, a shower curtain, a computer, a table, some chairs... '

'OK, Daisy, but I'm thinking of something we could buy right now.' With about €20.

'Oh right. Russian hamsters.'

As far as my children are concerned a house is not a home without Russian hamsters, but for the moment I resist. No, what I decide we must have, immediately, are scented candles and potpourri. I'm not sure why this conviction comes over me – maybe Martha Stewart has been tampering with my subconscious – but we head off to Casa, a scented candle shop conveniently situated opposite McDonald's.

On our return I wonder why I left all the sleeping bags and other things on the front lawn by an open window. Then I notice the smashed windows and the empty hall. Where have all the boxes of the kid's stuff gone? Finally it hits me. We've been burgled. They've taken Alice's birthday presents including her hammock from the garden. It's the hammock that flips me. In a split second I change from prison reform, Amnesty

International liberal into an ardent supporter of capital punishment for sheep rustling and hammock stealing.

'I'm going to the dogs' home and getting a Rottweiler,' is the first thing I say, which is a little unfair to Bibi, my beloved Pyrenean sheepdog, who I'm sure would have fought off the burglars. Her breed was awarded a special medal in World War One for bravery crossing enemy lines, and I'm sure Bibi would lay down her life for me. Though she's knee-high, bimbo-blonde and fluffy, and weighs 10 kilos, she's a sheepdog and in her mind things are black and white: either you're a sheep or a wolf. If you're a sheep she'll sacrifice her life, slobber on your best jeans and sleep in your bed after she's rolled in dead fish. If you're a wolf threatening her flock she'll kill you or die in the attempt. We're her favourite sheep and I'm sure she'd have defended our hammocks to the death. I should have called her Gelert.

Unfortunately my faithful hound wasn't there to guard the house; she'd come with us to choose scented candles. So I've separated from my husband, moved house and been burgled in the space of a day. I seem to be running through the list of Traumatic Life Experiences at an alarming rate. When things calm down, the kids want to know when we're getting the Rottweiler.

'What? I hate Rottweilers. They're killing machines.'

'But you promised. This is a difficult time for us too, Mum, it's not all about you, you know. I think the least you could do, now that you've torn the family apart, is get us a Rottweiler.'

'I will not succumb to emotional blackmail, Daisy.'

'What about Russian hamsters then?'

'Oh, OK.' Damn it, why did I say that? I *have* succumbed to emotional blackmail. I've let myself be persuaded that rodents are essential to the emotional well-being of my children. As we head off to the pet shop, I comfort myself with the thought that at €6 apiece, hamsters are cheaper than counselling.

'That one looks sweet.'

'But, Mummy, we need one *each*... '

So we go home with a cage full of the things, but they don't last long. As it turns out hamsters are killing machines, too. They sleep for months on end, wake up and try to murder each other, and then go straight back to sleep. On the plus side, they're a lot smaller than a Rottweiler.

WELCOME TO WILMAWORLD

I've had to put the surf idea on hold as winter is closing in. Some surfers keep going through the harsher conditions – hail and occasional snow, wild storms and closed bars. But no one in his or her right mind ever *learns* to surf in winter. I've decided to ignore general opinion that no 44-year-old woman in her right mind would attempt to learn to surf anyway. I'm not willing to give up on the idea; on the other hand, I am willing to wait until spring.

After the last few traumatic months, I have work to catch up on in the studio and I need to concentrate on the kids and do a bit of nest building in our new home, which quickly becomes known as the Addams Family Mansion.

I paint the walls blood red to make it more cosy and burn a lot of myrrh and frankincense until Daisy suggests that I might be getting carried away with the Morticia role. The house becomes a menagerie as my children use emotional blackmail to persuade me that they need not only Russian hamsters, but also cockatiels, dwarf rabbits, turtles and Siamese fighting fish to help them heal the scars of the break up.

Halloween falls neatly soon after the move and it seems like a good plan to throw a combined house-warming/*Night of the Living Dead* bash. As we've just moved in, the guests can believe that I'm about to install an Ikea kitchen and move in the rest of the furniture. (I have taken my share of stuff and have a fridge now, but as I've moved from a small, minimally decorated apartment to a rambling ruin, my few pieces of furniture don't make any impression.) I decorate the place with nettles and dead leaves from the garden and Mexican masks, which suits my melodramatic mood. Even if you know you're making the right decision, it's hard to walk out of a marriage without feeling emotionally raw around the edges.

As dusk falls the house fills with ghouls and zombies, werewolves, demons and vampires. It seems that everyone in the village has come, and those adults who haven't have kindly sent their children and teenage party animals who arrive in face paint and plastic rubbish bags and spray the house with fluorescent goo. Sacks of sweets and vats of wine are consumed, the house is trashed to the extent that I'm glad there was no furniture or shiny new kitchen, and the party becomes an annual fixture. Even if I try to cancel it, everyone still turns up, along with a few mysterious gatecrashers who only seem interested in the blood pudding on the buffet table.

I finally set up my studio in the basement. I start off in the sitting room, but glitter and feathers from my collages get in the food and onto everyone's clothes so we look like a family of glam rockers. My studio is not the clean white space some artists like to work in. I think you can tell a lot about an artist by looking in his or her studio, like studying the contents of a woman's handbag. If the studio is too clean and white it seems to me to indicate a control freak, so if you follow the logic that would make me the opposite – an out-of-control freak, maybe. I like to be able to lock myself in my studio, make a mess with my oil paint, talk to myself and sing along to Mexican love songs when I'm working without risking the ridicule of my children. I work in chaos and see what comes out of it. When magazines send photographers round, they always seem to want photos of my palette, which is encrusted with layers of brightly coloured paint several centimetres thick. My work jeans suffer the same fate and people sometimes try to buy them. I'd rather they concentrated on the paintings, but it's quite flattering all the same.

The basement is hung with cobwebs and carpeted with dead leaves blown in from the garden, ivy grows through the walls and strange fungi appear in the cracks. To say it's damp is an understatement; in heavy rain it floods and I have to work in wellingtons, catching pencils as they float around in 5 centimetres of water. There's a subterranean natural light from high windows facing up in to the garden, which are barred with wrought iron; shafts of sunlight catch the dust and glitter in the air. In some ways the dungeon-like atmosphere works well for me. It makes me paint in colours strong enough to fight through the stolen light. To get out of here I feel I have to produce something really beautiful, like an alchemist searching for the formula for gold.

I work alone apart from a rabbit and a pet rat, which the kids have installed down here, and other creatures that find their way in: large spiders, lizards, a stray hedgehog, or birds and bats. When I'm not working I'm quite sociable, but in the studio I become reclusive and very strange. My children treat me with extreme caution knowing that my sunny, charming nature undergoes a Jekyll-and-Hyde transformation when I'm painting. I turn into a psychotic megalomaniac: I talk to myself and shout at my paintings. I have been known to smash furniture and rip canvases apart with my bare hands when a colour isn't working for me.

Colour is important to me; my paintings are always very vividly coloured. They're also always of women. They might be portraits or self-portraits, madonnas or cancan dancers, Amazon warriors, silent movie stars or nuns, but always women.

As a child I started painting princesses and goddesses and never really stopped. As a teenager my bedroom was plastered with posters not of rock stars but Toulouse-Lautrec courtesans, Pre-Raphaelite redheads, Mucha and Klimt. I was disappointed to discover that all these images were painted by men, and women were at best artists' wives, mistresses and muses, models or prostitutes. I wanted to paint women from a woman's perspective, often using myself as artist, model and, in Neo Naturist days, the canvas.

Unfortunately I think my attitude spoiled the notion of art as fun in our household. I'll never forget finding Daisy at the age of about five tearing a painting of a princess into shreds sobbing melodramatically, 'I can't go on! This is not good enough to sell.'

I'm not keen on my own children being in the studio, so you can imagine how I feel when complete strangers barge in unannounced after reading my name in the local paper or an interiors magazine. I think it's a cultural difference; in France artists often sell from their studio, or have a little gallery attached, so the studio is expected to be guest friendly. Mine isn't; even my children have to knock. None of the visitors ever buy, either. If they did I might be more inclined to roll out the red carpet. One afternoon a group of well-dressed ladies, who clearly subscribe to *Maisons du Sud Ouest,* come round out of the blue expecting a free lecture and a cup of afternoon tea. They find me dripping with paint, my hands are covered in gold leaf, my hair is tied up with a piece of fish net and I'm sewing a dead moth onto a collage. Welcome to Wilmaworld.

NOW OR NEVER

Spring comes, the bitter oranges ripen on the tree outside my bedroom window, the bars re-open, the village emerges from hibernation and the ocean changes from seething mass of dark water and foam into a sheet of glittering turquoise. I come out of my cave rubbing my eyes in the sunlight and decide I can't put off the moment of truth any longer. It's time to get in the water.

So what do I need to become a surfer? Looking at myself I'd say a lot more testosterone, a deep bronze tan, a few tattoos, rippling biceps. Those can come later, first of all I need a board. I can see that even this is complicated. I can imagine the reaction if I walked into a surf shop and said, 'Hello, I want to become a surfer like you guys. Can I have a board please, and one of those stringy things to tie it to my ankle? Oh, and a block of your finest Sex Wax.'

Mr Zog's Sex Wax – 'best for your stick' – has no particular aphrodisiac properties as far as I know, although the coconut smell might be a turn-on for Barry Manilow fans. It's what you put on your board to stop you slithering off when you stand up. I don't know how well it works; I have been tempted to add a drop of superglue to it from time to time. I'm sure wax is only called Sex Wax, Kangaroo Poo and Mrs Palmers Mighty Mounds to discourage women from learning to surf. So for a while I do nothing about getting a board. I've begun to think that perhaps I'm crazy and I should buy a badminton set instead, until one night I have a stroke of luck in a bar in San Sebastián.

Spain was the furthest I ever went as a child. We would set out from London and drive south for three days to visit friends in a medieval hill town in the sierra outside Madrid, stopping at every cathedral for a lecture on Gothic architecture and the Spanish Inquisition from my father and eating delicacies like chorizo, anchovy-stuffed olives and suckling pigs that hadn't yet reached the London suburbs. It all seemed very exotic, and I still get excited crossing the border. I love the idea that in ten minutes I can be in another country. I could go to Pamplona and relive Ernest Hemingway's *Fiesta*, get drunk and fall in love with a young bullfighter, leaving a trail of broken hearts and hangovers in my wake. Or I could keep driving across to La Mancha or Extremadura on the way to Andalucía for a flamenco festival, then on to Morocco and the Sahara.

There may be no borders in the European Community now, but I wouldn't try telling that to the Guardia Civil standing halfway across the Bidasoa River with machine guns and chain tyre shredders. The border is long and winds through the mountains; you can walk on the paths used by refugees from the Spanish Civil War going one way, and refugees escaping from the Nazis the other way. The old smuggling posts where you could once buy contraband brandy and cigars have mushroomed into supermarkets and shopping malls built incongruously on the mountainside. Sunday shoppers come over from France for all those weekend essentials: chorizo, Rioja, ornamental sabres, flamenco dresses, paella dishes and cheap sunglasses. I often go over for a bottle of wine and a flamenco postcard just because I can and it's so much more exciting than the 7-Eleven.

Tonight I've come down for tapas with my Australian friends Phil and Trudi. There was a time when a piece of tuna and an artichoke heart speared together on a toothpick seemed exciting, but the standards have gotten higher. San Sebastián has the best tapas in Spain and we're looking for the bar with the best tapas in San Sebastián, so we're on a mission to find the best tapas in the world. It's a bit like the quest for the Perfect Wave, but less energetic.

Our expectations may be high, but the Bar Bergara doesn't let us down; it's a temple to tapas (or *pintxos* as they're called in Basque). The counter is groaning with platters of crab meat, octopus and tuna; serrano hams and chorizo hang from the ceiling. There are tapas trophies above the bar, and backlit neon photos of tapas cover the walls. A laminated menu describes the prize-winning morsels you are about to eat - foie gras with grapes soaked in port, duck pickled in Calvados with pine nuts, false lasagna of anchovy and crab. It's all washed down in time honoured fashion with Rioja and cigar smoke.

Phil Grace is one of those surfers who has lived the Endless Summer dream of every teenage boy with a Quiksilver T-shirt and a block of wax. He's surfed all over the world since the

1960s, discovering waves that had never been surfed, hanging out with world champions and legendary surf bums like Miki Dora. He lives between Olatua and Australia now, and shapes boards in Hossegor for pro surfers. At some point during the evening, he says he'd like to commission a painting. I stop with a marinated octopus tentacle halfway to my mouth, a little cartoon light bulb appears above my head.

'Would you like to swap it for a board?' I say as casually as I can.

'Sure,' he says, sounding a little surprised. 'I didn't know you surfed.'

Of course he knows I don't. You only have to look at a person's arms to know whether they surf or not, and I have skinny little arms, stressed by lifting heavy things like large paintbrushes or pints of Guinness.

'I don't – yet. But I thought I might start. It's now or never.' I go through the clichés: Never too late, *carpe diem*, life begins at 40, or perhaps 44 in my case. 'You don't think I'm too old, do you?'

It's a loaded question and I'm slightly dreading the answer. I'm half expecting him to laugh in my face and tell me I'm way too old, especially as he's witnessed my lack of balance on dry land after a few Riojas.

'No, if you want to do it, go for it. You're quite fit, aren't you?'

'Oh yes.' I think that's the Rioja talking. It's all relative, isn't it? I'm probably not fit compared to the pro surfers Phil hangs out with in Hossegor. But if you compared me to that table of old men in berets smoking cigars in the corner or to the regulars at the bar in the Colony Room on a Friday night, I'd be doing OK.

'You'll want something quite long and stable if you're just starting. You probably don't want to go in waves over, say, two metres, do you?'

Two metres? He must be kidding.

'Let's say more like two centimetres... ' I'm not ambitious, I don't see myself as a big-wave hell woman. The bigger the board the smaller the waves you can surf it on, and the more chance you have of standing up on it, so I'm thinking the bigger the better. It gets to sound more like a life raft than a surfboard as we go on, until in the end Trudi interrupts, laughing, 'Don't forget that you have to be able to pick it up, Wilma.'

I wake up the next morning, not regretting the board, but very much regretting the nightcap in the Bar Basque. I promise myself that if I survive this hangover I'll join a gym and never drink absinthe again. By lunchtime I've commuted my sentence and decide to go to the pool and only drink absinthe on special occasions.

But there's the usual catch 22: how do you get to look good in your swimsuit before you've done the swimming? This isn't the Crouch End lido. I've always thought it's a sensible idea to take your worn-out old swimsuit to the pool – the one you're just about to chuck out because the elastic has gone and it's getting a bit see-through. Old swimsuit, big mistake because the pool is where the Beautiful People go to stay beautiful when it's too cold for the beach or too flat to surf. I understand half an hour too late that you need a full body wax and a session on the sunbed before you come to do your lengths in Biarritz.

I try wearing black goggles and a flowery plastic hat, but it's worse and people penetrate the disguise and think I'm slightly crazy: *'Oh là là, les Anglaises, comme elles sont originales!'*

A few months later Phil brings the board around. It's a shiny, white, 9-foot 8-inch-long board with a logo of a man hanging ten on the front as inspiration. He did offer me the chance of painting the board, in which case I might have put a woman hanging ten – even more inspirational.

'When you surf this board, you have to step back a bit to turn it, then move your weight forward a couple of steps, then to hang five you want to cross step to the nose and...'

I feel a bit task overloaded.

'Wait a minute. I have to learn to stand up first.'

'Oh, yes, I forgot.' He laughs. 'That's not a bad idea. Start in the white water, have a bit of fun.'

I even have to ask him how to wax it. I'm taken back to when Daisy was born and I had to ring for a nurse to show me how to change my baby's first nappy. For a few days I'm too nervous even to touch the board, I leave it in the middle of the room and walk round it, thinking, oh fuck, what have I done?

THE WORST SURFER IN THE WORLD

I wait until the weather's warm and choose a day when I can hardly see a ripple on the water to launch the board. I pick a long sandy beach where I can stay in my depth and close to the lifeguard tower so I can be rescued if the worst comes to the worst.

My friends on the beach agree that the swell is somewhere between 30 centimetres and 'nothing at all out there'. But it's amazing how much bigger waves look when they're breaking over your head. It's a perspective thing: as an artist I should understand it. But it's hard to focus on the vanishing point when you're in a state of primal fear.

I'm usually quite happy in waves. I've always enjoyed splashing around, diving under them, getting washed onto the beach with my bikini round my feet. But this is different; it feels like trying to swim with a coffee table tied to my ankle. To make things worse there are a lot of other people in the water with coffee tables tied to their ankles. It's like a floating furniture showroom. Some people are standing on their tables, some are sitting astride them scanning the horizon for waves, others are lying down paddling. But I don't even seem able to manage paddling; I spend most of the time flailing around in the shallows like a beached whale, waiting for the board to hit me on the head.

The great Hawaiian surfer Duke Kahanamoku once said, 'Out of the water I am nothing.' For me it's the opposite. *In* the water I am nothing. Out of the water I may not be everything. I may have a few unachieved ambitions, unsolved problems and unpaid debts, but at least I can stand up for God's sake.

Surfing is meant to be rejuvenating, but this is ridiculous – I've regressed 40 years. I feel like a frustrated toddler. When I stumble back up the beach an hour or two later, my children are waiting. But they're not about to pop open the bubbly and throw a garland of hibiscus flowers round my neck.

'*Trop nul*. You're CRAP.'

'Yes, well, I think the swell has got up a bit; maybe I should wait until it drops. I'm not sure if it's safe to be out there.'

I turn round, look at the water and do a double take. It's hard to believe that the sparkling calm sea I'm looking at is the terrifying maelstrom I've just come out of. I'm trying to work out this discrepancy when someone brings a golden retriever down to the beach, puts it on a board and pushes it into a wave.

'Hey, Mum, how come that dog surfs better than you?' Nat asks.

Everyone laughs. Then the dog jumps elegantly off the board in the shore break, shakes its silky blond hair and runs up the beach like a *Baywatch* extra.

'But it really does. Why is that?'

That's the trouble with teaching your children moral values. You keep telling them how important it is to tell the truth, and what do they do? Throw it back in your face just when you least need to hear it. I put on the most grown-up, superior voice I can muster.

'Firstly, Nat, the dog has probably been surfing longer than I have. Secondly, it has four legs – *and a tail* – which obviously makes it a lot easier to balance.'

I mean, I don't want to accuse the dog of cheating, but I bet I could surf if I had four legs.

This goes on all summer. I'm determined to keep going, but I hit my first major obstacle before I even get my hair wet. The first thing surfers will tell you is this: 'When you want to stand up, you just do a little press-up. Try it on the beach first.'

The problem is that I've never done 'a little press-up' in my life. I thought that having reached 44, I might never have to. I've always subscribed to the convenient theory that it's good to stay healthy, but if you spend too much time worrying about your body, your mind might wither up... and after all, you can always wear loose clothes and take them off in the dark. If men only want you for your body they're shallow and worthless; we don't care about their bodies, do we? I personally do, but only from an artistic point of view...

Now that I live in the land of the Beautiful People, I'm wondering if brain over brawn is a bit of old-school feminist brainwashing sponsored by dungaree companies. What I'm searching for is the middle ground between body-as-enemy-of-the-mind and pole-dancing-as-empowerment feminism.

And it's not just my biceps holding me back. When you're grown up – I use that term loosely – you're not used to falling over. Once in a while I might trip over my high-heeled flip-flops while executing a complex salsa move after too much rosé, but that's not enough to prepare me for entire afternoons face-planting, bellyflopping and catapulting into the water over and over again like a B-movie stuntman, then having to apologise to elegant, naked French women as I plough into their children and poodles in the shore break.

Also, as a grown up you want to feel in control of things, or at least preserve that illusion in front of your children, but in the water I am totally out of control. 'It's all right, everyone has to learn sometime,' people tell me sympathetically.

The trouble is that everyone else seems to have gone through the learning process 40 years before me. Further out there may be grown ups on grown-up waves, but here in the waist-deep white wash the average age of the surfers is about six. They're used to falling over, they're used to not being in control, they're used to crying when they can't get something right. I cry pretty easily: Bette Davis movies, country-and-western songs and bank statements can all reduce me to tears. But it's a bit embarrassing to be caught sobbing with frustration on the beach, with bruised knees and water dripping from my nose.

'You're the worst surfer in the world, Mum,' Nat says to me cheerfully one morning. He doesn't really say it as an insult; he's not trying to deliver the *coup de grâce* to my wounded ego. He says it as if he's been thinking about it in the night and that maybe it's a rather impressive fact that could get me a place in the *Guinness World Records* alongside the biggest cupcake ever baked, the world's smelliest cheese and the woman with the longest toenails. He's only young, so I can't really expect him to understand the mid-life crisis psychology behind my need to reinvent myself as a surf goddess. He can't imagine being a forty-something woman whose life is in a state of chaos that can only be made meaningful by learning to stand up on a piece of fibreglass in the Bay of Biscay.

'Thanks, Nat.'

I think about his comment. Could anyone *technically* be worse than me? I'd like to think so, but it's hard to see how. I can't stand up, I can't even take a wave lying down and I don't seem to be able to stop the board jumping up out of the water and whacking me over the head. There are probably other people who would share the podium with me, but that's not the point. 'The best surfer in the world is the one having most fun' is a cornerstone of feel-good surfie philosophy. So does that mean the worst surfer in the world is the one having least fun... and is *that* me?

At first I was OK with my lack of progress. I thought to myself, I'll laugh about this in a couple of weeks when I'm out there with the boys. But the weeks have turned into months, and the novelty is wearing off. It's not just that I don't improve; I feel I'm falling apart after a series of accidents that could be used to illustrate a book called *How Not To Surf*.

Rule 1: *Never put your board between you and the wave.*

I fractured my collarbone and ended up with my arm in a sling before I took that rule seriously.

Rule 2: *Never grab the leash – the surfer's umbilical cord that attaches her or his ankle to the board.*

Broken finger caused by pure vanity. I wasn't exactly carving it up, in fact I wasn't even standing up, but I was doing pretty well until someone got out a camera. I lost concentration, trying to simultaneously smile sweetly, pull my bikini top back on and pick a lump of tar out of my hair. I let go of my board. I looked up to see it heading straight for a naked man splashing happily in the foam. I know you should never, ever grab your leash, but I couldn't live with the guilt of castrating an innocent naturist, so I did. This is why you never grab the leash: the weight of the board combined with some physics equation to do with the force of ocean waves compared to the strength of the cartilage in your little finger means that you will either break or lose the finger and never be able to drink tea politely again.

Rule 3: *Never take your eyes off the board.*

Big bruise on my jaw just before a trip to London. Friends were worried; they assumed that I was dating a Basque rugby man with anger-management problems. When I told them the truth, they were even more worried.

Rule 4: *Never run around the ramparts of Spanish hill villages after too many sherries.*

Sprained ankle during après-surf relaxation that ended up in the casualty department.

As a result of the injuries, I accept a compromise and buy myself a boogie board – a short foam board, which is surfed lying down, cutting out a lot of stress. (Although you risk being referred to as a speed bump, a sponger or a turtle rooter by stand up snobs.) Does it really matter if I'm vertical or horizontal? Boogie boarding doesn't seem to be quite how I remembered it from my days in Lyme Regis. I am not going to get away with standing in waist-deep water and letting the white water carry me in to the beach. This is only acceptable around here if you're under three or over 80. I'm expected to kit out in heavy-duty fins, neoprene ankle socks and to paddle way out to the peak. Oh, and that's after getting in the water which is not so easy because fins make you walk like a slightly drunk penguin. Someone gives me the useful tip that it's cooler to walk into the water backwards. Maybe, except that you can't see where you're going. I suspect that spectators just find it funnier seeing people fall over backwards.

I only try boogie boarding once, on a day so calm that it's hard to tell where the wave is meant to be breaking. After flapping around like a demented penguin for the afternoon without even catching a wave, I lose both my big toenails. This is because I refuse to wear the neoprene ankle socks with a bikini. I'm too vain, or perhaps I've been infected by a strain of contagious French chic. I give up, enrol at the local sports physiotherapy centre when my shoulder gives out and leave the board standing in the living room like a totem to my failure.

The Beautiful People get used to me limping around the village with my arm in a sling and my toenails held on with superglue.

'How's the surfing going?' they ask sympathetically. I'm not sure what the French for mid-life crisis is, *crise des femmes d'un certain âge* or something, but I'm sure that's what they're thinking. I remember seeing a film about F. Scott Fitzgerald's wife Zelda, who decided to become a ballerina in her thirties and practised obsessively night and day. Eventually she was dragged off to a sanatorium, tutu and pointe shoes under her straitjacket. The ghost of Christmas Future. I can see myself being escorted away by the men in white coats, wetsuit under my straitjacket, people whispering, 'So sad, she thought she could learn to surf when she was 44 and she couldn't even do the press-up.'

MAMMA MIA

On midsummer night I'm invited to celebrate the solstice with some Swedish friends. It's the first day of a three-month heat wave. The whole of Olatua is there, and everyone arrives paralysed by the 40-degree-Celsius heat.

'Have you got a cold drink?'

Our hostess, Susanne, looks like a Nordic goddess in a crown of white flowers.

'Here.' She hands me a glass. 'Home-made schnapps.'

Impossible to refuse. It's ice cold, fruit flavoured and really refreshing. It's also about 40-per-cent proof. But everyone's too hot to care; we're knocking it back like shandy. Soon we're celebrating the solstice in traditional Viking style, eating Ikea pickled herring, dancing to Abba.

'Look.' Phil Jarratt is demonstrating surf techniques. 'You just do a little press-up.' (You can never escape the little press-up, even after midnight.) 'And you jump up like this. Now, if you want to hang ten, cross step, another cross step... '. Phil is an Australian writer who set up the cult surf mag *Tracks* in the 1970s, then became the editor of Australian *Playboy*.

Although he is still surrounded by bikini models in his new job at Quiksilver it's hard to imagine him in Hugh Hefner pyjamas and dressing gown as he hangs ten on Susanne's coffee table in board shorts and a faded Bintang Beer T-shirt. This T-shirt is a statement piece in the surf world – it says, 'I went to Indonesia, I took waves, I drank beer, I am core.'

If I can't do a press-up sober, I'm hardly likely to be able to do one after five glasses of schnapps. So I wander off and go back to dancing to Abba, which I find is something you can only do when you *have* had at least five glasses of schnapps.

After a few more shots, I become morose. It's funny how meaningful Abba can seem at three in the morning. It must be something they put in the herring. I'm not the dancing queen, I'm not a super trouper, I'm not only 17, and I don't feel like I win when I lose. Damn it, I can't even surf. It's my Waterloo. Can you hear the bongo drums, Fernando?

I bump into a friend, Mike, who's been surfing for 50 years. To explain how hard core he is: he's the kind of man who goes to Nicaragua to surf *because* there's a war raging, which will mean that the waves will be empty.

'How's it going?'

'Miserable. I can't surf. I can't stand up. It's been months now and I just can't do it.' He laughs.

'Why are you so stressed out? You're only having fun, aren't you?'

'Fun? Listen to the music.'

As 'The Winner Takes It All' blasts out I can't help feeling the lyrics are directed at me. I'm not the winner, I'm the loser who can't even do a simple little thing like a press-up. I've always thought it weird that Abba made platinum-selling records about the Napoleonic wars and the Mexican revolution – now I understand, the lyrics are not about war and revolution at all – they're about *me* learning to surf.

'It's not much fun when you're underwater with your leash wrapped round your neck, inhaling seawater and swallowing small jellyfish,' I continue.

Worse than that I'm terrified that I may have left it too late. There are some things I can accept that I'm too old to do: becoming a prima ballerina, skateboarding, wearing a T-shirt with 'Nutty Tart' written on it. I can't accept that I'm too old to learn to surf, although I can feel my body strength seeping away minute by minute – or is that the schnapps?

'Come over here, have another drink and I'll explain,' I say to Mike.

If I were a successful businessman I could just run off with my secretary or buy a red sports car. But life is always so much tougher for women, isn't it? I can't do either of those things, so I have to take up a profoundly macho extreme sport instead. I'm not just frolicking in the foam, I'm confronting my mortality. (Never a good idea when listening to Abba.) I try to explain this to Mike whose form is getting blurred around the edges by now.

'Mike, don't you get it? I thought I was the dancing queen but actually I'm Napoleon fucking Bonaparte.'

MY LIFE AS A
GUINEA PIG

A few weeks after my midsummer meltdown, I see my friend Johanna for coffee.

'God, I wish I was fit like you.' It's Sunday morning and I've caught her between a 10-kilometre run and a surf. She's caught me between an Alka-Seltzer and a siesta.

Johanna is another recent arrival in town, a Swedish free-ski pro who decided to swap endless winter for Endless Summer. She's everything you'd expect of a Nordic snow queen: glamorous, blonde, tanned, total athlete. After years on the free-ski world tour, she's come down from the mountains to the ocean and she's learning to surf – with a little more success than me, partly because she lives with a surf instructor. Christophe Reinhardt is a former national champion and local big-wave hell man, and he's everything you'd expect from a French wave hero: year-round tan, sexy accent, outrageous flirt. His father was one of the first surfers in Biarritz in the 1950s and took him out on a board at the tender age of four

– maybe Christophe thought he'd started too late, he took his own son Bruno out at two.

Apart from being French national champion and surfing waves up to 7-metres high around the world, he also competed in world championships of tandem surf in Hawaii. This involves a man and woman surfing a long heavy board together, the man lifting his partner above his head so she can perform elegant arabesque-like movements. You can buy a postcard of him, a garland of hibiscus flowers round his neck and his daughter Valentine balanced delicately above his head on one arm, in the village *bar-tabac*.

Walking into the living room, you're left in no doubt that you're in a surfer's house. The furniture is made from driftwood and there are boards everywhere. Pride of place goes to his collection of red Lightning Bolt boards from Hawaii, which he surfed at famous breaks like Sunset and Pipeline in the 1970s; big-wave riders' trophies hanging on the walls like big-game hunters' antelope heads.

I always seem to bump into Johanna when I have a hangover; whether this is a coincidence or a lifestyle thing I couldn't really say, but today is no exception. I spent the previous evening with French friends; it was meant to be quite low key, but the social etiquette of Biarritz dictates that it's extremely impolite to leave a dinner party before two in the morning or to refuse a drink while still standing. I'm suffering for my perfect manners.

'I wish I was fit like you' is a Pavlovian reaction to seeing her. What it really means is: I wish I wasn't about to die of Côtes du Rhône overdose, and I wouldn't mind looking like you in a bikini – if there was a bikini on the whole of planet surf that I could squeeze into. (In the rest of the world I'm a medium, size 12, average kind of woman, but in Biarritz this converts to XL for most things and off the scale for bikini tops.)

'You always say that when we meet. You really mean it, don't you?'

Do I? I look at her, and then I have an out-of-body look at myself. I can't remotely imagine being 'fit like her'. She's a professional sportswoman, she's spent the last ten years competing on the free-ski tour, flying round the world for competitions and photo shoots, stunt skiing for movies and heli-skiing in the Andes and Himalayas. I'm an artist and I've spent the last ten years pretending to be an earth mother, growing vegetables and cooking baby food. She's a Bond Girl and I'm hovering somewhere between the walking wounded and the living dead. But I don't want to sound insincere.

'Yes, I guess so. It would be nice to be fit and healthy... and... stuff.' Swedish, blonde, tanned, powder-snow queen.

'Well that's perfect because I'm thinking about becoming a personal trainer and I need a guinea pig.'

'Oh yes, that's a good idea.' What am I saying?

'I'll go and get my questionnaire.'

This might be a good moment to make a quick getaway. I look towards the door, but Christophe is doing pull-ups on a driftwood beam, blocking my escape route.

'First question. What kind of training do you do at the moment?' Training? I look blank.

'For instance, when did you last go for a run?'

I think back. Probably that time in London when I nearly missed the 134 bus on my way to a drinking club in Soho.

'Not for a while.'

'A month? A year? Five years? *Ten years?*'

'Oh no, not *ten years*. Really, maybe, thinking about it, more like... never.'

'Oh. OK let's move on to the next question. What other sports do you do regularly?'

'That's another no I'm afraid.'

'In the past?

I think back. Nothing springs to mind. I think further back.

I have had my moments. I went to a swimming club with my sister when I was a kid. I was 12 and she was nine; the lanes went from one to eight, hot to hopeless. She was in lane one, I was in lane eight. I'd stand there spluttering and coughing, wondering what part of 'I can't do front crawl' the coach didn't understand, getting a bit of vicarious pleasure watching my sister beat teenage boys in butterfly races. It wasn't that I was really bad at swimming, but I could only swim on my back. Then there was Mr Fish's tennis club where I had the honour of being paired with the pro's son. He usually beat me, which would have been fine because he obviously had a bit of an advantage... except that he was five and I was 14.

'Well, you must at least have done some sport at college?'

Johanna's making the mistake of comparing a Swedish sports college to St Martins College of Art in the days of the New Romantics. To say that there wasn't a fitness culture is an understatement – if you weren't actually on drugs you were expected to at least make the effort to look fashionably wasted. Healthy tan was out; consumptive pallor was in. My look was the ghost of Marie Antoinette, so even if I had been tempted to get sporty, it would have been hard in 12-centimetre-high heels and a crinoline. My only sporting achievement was winning the three-legged beer race round Soho organised by the student union. It wasn't very different from any other day as far as I remember except that I had one ankle tied to someone else's ankle. My time at college was like an endless beer race in fancy dress. The girls dressed in Elizabethan costumes, feather hats and Oxfam vintage. The boys dressed as pirates and eighteenth-century dandies and went out with each other, leaving the girls wondering why all the best men were gay. Were we really expected to go out with the straight boys in painting and sculpture who wore boiler suits?

But I had a secret life, like Catherine Deneuve in *Belle de Jour*, only a bit less chic and pervy. In the summer I disappeared from the London scene. I put mothballs in my Taboo wardrobe and hitch-hiked to Lyme Regis, where my grandparents had a house on the sea front, to go windsurfing. I spent the whole summer either in a wetsuit or a plain-clothes disguise of stripy T-shirts, nerdy jeans and oilskins from the local yacht shop. This was before the surf clothes industry took off – in Dorset at least. I could have bought a T-shirt with 'Windsurfers Do It Standing Up' printed on it, but I resisted the temptation. I drank cider with the windsurfers, lifeboat men and mackerel fishermen and went to events like the Whitchurch Canonicorum village fête or the Lyme carnival conger-cuddling contest. I'd get postcards from Soho about ultra-hip clubs and parties I'd missed, and wonder whether I would fit back into my old life. But once I got to the North Circular on the outskirts of London at the beginning of September, I instinctively reached for the Yardley powder compact and the Holly Red lipstick. I put a rinse in my hair to cover the blonde streaks and dusted off my hat collection. There was a moment when I could have turned, maybe if I'd fallen in love with a local windsurfer rather than another gay New Romantic, but I could never have got my head around the sportswear.

Instead, I converted my Lyme Regis persona into performance art. I entered Andrew Logan's drag beauty contest – the Alternative Miss World – as Miss Windsurfer. I then went on to win Miss St Martins as Miss Fish, dressed – or undressed – as a mermaid in body-painted scales and a tail so tight I had to be lifted on and off the stage. One of the judges was Quentin Crisp, an icon in the gay rights movement, but not so well known in the extreme sports world. I decide my beauty pageant triumphs probably don't count as sport either.

'A bit of windsurfing twenty-five years ago.'

'Oh great, I tried that in Hawaii. It's fun, isn't it?'

'Yeah, well, Lyme Regis isn't quite the same... '

I remember the scuba course I took in Dingle. I'm not sure if scuba is technically a sport, but it's definitely Bond Girl training. The main things you have to do are sink and move as little as possible, so Johanna and I agree that if I remember that the aims of surfing are exactly the opposite to scuba, it might help.

Johanna might be regretting her choice of guinea pig, but she must feel better when I get on the floor to do the press-up test because I do a pretty good impression of a guinea pig. I lie there contemplating the physical impossibility of raising my bodyweight on my flimsy front paws, making little squeaky noises. 'Give me carrots. Give me hay. Give me beer.' As I said, having made it through four decades plus without ever having to do a press-up, I thought I had dodged the bullet. If I hadn't had my revelation on the westernmost beach, I might have.

'You can start now,' she says.

'Er... I already have. I think that's it.' Christophe stifles a giggle as he walks past looking for more weights for the dumb-bells.

'Oh.' There's a pause. She puts it as gently as she can. 'I think you're going to have to develop a *little* more upper-body strength if you want to learn to surf.'

You don't say no to a Bond Girl, and somehow I find that I've agreed to go jogging the next morning. I go home and announce this to the children. They look at me in disbelief.

'What do you mean?' one of them asks after a long silence.

I repeat the sentence loudly and slowly like an English tourist in a foreign restaurant.

'But, Mum, do you know how to run? Have you ever done it?'

'Yeah, of course she has. Remember that time she almost missed the bus on her way to the Colony Room?'

'There's absolutely no reason I shouldn't go for a run. But can someone lend me their sports kit because I'm not sure if you can do it in flip-flops?'

JUST DO IT

I buy myself a pair of white nylon trainers.

'New shoes, Mum?' Daisy asks pointedly.

'Yes, do you like them?'

'They're an insult to fashion. I hope you're not going to wear them in the village.'

That's what happens when your children live in a chic French beach resort – they don't just learn the language, they learn that way of eyeing your shoes as if you'd bought them with dog shit already attached.

'I'm going *running*, darling, I need the LunarEclipse sole,' I say as snottily as I can.

Running's not so hard. You just put one foot in front of the other and try not to trip over your laces or fall into a pothole. I do, however, encounter a bit of resistance from friends and family in London.

'Running? Are you sure that's safe at your age?' my father asks, rather hypocritically considering that, to everyone's surprise, he took up windsurfing at 55. He used to love cruising around Lyme Bay in a sailor's hat with sunglasses tied to his head and only gave up when he got a hip replacement.

I have to fight the theory that jogging can seriously damage your health and that I might become one of those bitchy cheerleaders in teen movies if I develop biceps and toned calves.

My sister is with my dad on this. 'You might get shin shock or have a heart attack. You're not becoming a body fascist, are you?'

It's a steep learning curve and I get aches and pains in muscles I didn't know I had. The children come home to find me collapsed on the sofa smothered in Tiger Balm, moaning softly as I sip on a vitamin supplement.

'Just having a little siesta... I think I overdid it last night.' Why am I pretending to have a hangover instead of admitting that I got carried away with my sit-ups?

'But you're not even drinking.' Oh damn, caught out, I'm on a dry month. Maybe I'm getting a little carried away with the idea of New Improved Wilma.

'OK, I went to the gym. It hurts. Is it really that funny, Nat?'

I don't know why my son should find this quite so hilarious. Perhaps after all these years of me teaching him stuff, sharing my superior wisdom and generally acting as if I'm an omnipotent infallible creature it's fun for him to see me struggling to do something, like a press-up, that seems so ridiculously simple to him. I gradually work my way from walking a couple of kilometres with a bit of girly trotting on downhill sections to running 6 kilometres along the coast two or three times a week.

Johanna, as I said, has moved to Olatua from Verbier in the Swiss Alps. The world of extreme skiing does have its macho side, and she was one of only five women on the free-ski world tour. But most women who live in ski resorts ski, and she's shocked by how few women surf on the coast. She may live with a surfer who has a shelf of trophies, but Johanna has no intention of joining the Surf Widows. We're not talking about women sitting in freezing car parks with a Cornish pasty and a Thermos of tea, which is something I've tried and tested. No, the Biarritz Surf Widows are a glamorous tribe, a bit like rock stars' wives. They actually seem to enjoy sitting in beachside cafes eating oysters washed down with chilled Chablis rather than riding the wild wave with their husbands. We both agree that this is a disturbing situation and action needs to be taken. Apart from anything else it would be nice to have a few more women in the water. The waves themselves are intimidating enough; the feeling that you've walked into a men's locker room is the bitter icing on the cake.

The idea of the surf club comes up one day when Johanna and I are running along the cliffs. The sun is setting over the mountains in Spain and a full moon is rising over Biarritz. I'm feeling inspired and full of endorphins, if slightly breathless, as if I'm in a Nike ad. I can almost see 'Just Do It' written in the jet streams over the ocean. Johanna is jogging alongside, calm and composed, as if she could just keep going all the way to San Sebastián for tapas if she felt like it. She's told me you should never be too out of breath to talk while you're running, so I'm letting her do most of the talking while I stick to monosyllabic responses.

'I thought we could set up a surf club for women, do you think it's a good idea?'

'Yes.'

'I'm sure there are lots of women your age around here who want to learn to surf.'

'Yes.'

'There's no reason you can't start in your forties.'

'No.'

'We could start in spring when it gets a bit warmer. We don't need to start in the middle of winter, do we?'

'No.'

'In the meantime, we could do an evening at our place. I thought it could be a sushi night. I've always wanted to make sushi, haven't you?'

'Yes.' Hang on, shouldn't that have been a no? I thought sushi just came like that – stuffed and rolled and ready trimmed.

Bond Girl, superwoman, now Domestic Goddess. Not only can she ski off walls of ice and do press-ups, she can bake Swedish saffron buns, knit Norwegian jumpers and, apparently, make sushi. You know that thing where you're meant to hang out with women in your own league so you don't feel bad about yourself? I think I fucked up.

Johanna explains her Domestic Goddess tendency to me. 'When I'd been on an extreme ski trip, it was nice to do something really different when I got home, like knit a jumper or bake bread.'

I can see it's a question of perspective. It depends whether you've spent the last ten years stunt skiing in the Himalayas or being an earth mother in an Irish fishing village. The ski trip sounds like more of a novelty to me.

Despite my confusion about the sushi, I think it's a great idea. We have the coach lined up already. Apart from being big-wave hell man, Christophe has his own surf school and, as he is always happy to admit, women and waves are his favourite things. So the idea of a women-only surf club is not entirely unattractive to him.

GEISHA NIGHTS

Making sushi isn't as hard as you'd think; it's a lot harder. Definitely a recipe for a geisha with a slow love life. It's like a *Blue Peter* craft thing that doesn't turn out how it should: you end up with rice in your hair, seaweed in your eyebrows and squid under your fingernails. I spend a few hours working on the sushi with Johanna before everyone arrives: sculpting rice, slicing bait, doing origami with sheets of seaweed. And then just when I've constructed the perfect California roll, someone comes in, pops it in her mouth and says, 'Yummy.' Yummy? That was a work of art and she didn't even look at it before she destroyed it! The women arrive alone, as this is a women's surf club. Christophe puts on an apron and serves the sake. Biarritz is a cosmopolitan place, it's on a surf-orientated ley line that attracts people from all over the world, and so it's a very international group of women who have mainly ended up here because their husbands surf. Most of us are in our forties and most of us have children, so the conversation swings magnetically in that direction.

'Why doesn't anyone ever tell you how hard it's going to be looking after kids?'

I'm talking to Taryn who is from Idaho. Like me, she wanted to have kids without turning into the illustration in the childcare manual. She's lived in California, Tokyo, Paris, Dakar and the Alps, and she's finding the school run a little monotonous. I think about her question: would anyone have children if they knew how difficult it would be? Or would the whole human race suffer the same fate as the Shakers, making furniture instead of making love and becoming extinct?

And *why* doesn't anyone tell the truth about childbirth either? I'm blaming women for the conspiracy of silence; it's one of the few things you can't blame on men. Maybe it's because it doesn't occur to a woman to mention the downside of childbirth to someone until that someone is pregnant, and then it's too late.

I went down the natural childbirth route: obviously as an aspiring earth mother I had no choice. Beanbags, essential oils, raspberry leaf tea and ambient music are very nice, and I know that women have been using these aids since the beginning of time, but they have also been suffering and dying in childbirth. It still hurts. By the time I got into transition, I'd realised that whale music is not a painkiller and I'd changed my mind completely about the whole thing. Transition is the stage just before you start to push. There's a medical explanation why women become abusive during childbirth; personally I think we're just making the most of our last opportunity to behave like bitches before turning into angelic madonna figures.

'I'm not doing this, let me go home,' I screamed. 'Make it stop. Give me drugs, anything you've got: epidurals, pethidine, morphine, your finest A-class washed down with a strawberry margarita.'

'Oh no, too late for that now, dear. According to my notes you chose a natural birth plan.' But it's all worth it, because at the end of it you get: 1. a baby and 2. some great dinner party anecdotes, as we are proving tonight.

Christophe probably started off thinking, 'Cool, I get to spend the evening surrounded by beautiful women who are making sushi for me,' but Christophe's dream turns into a nightmare as the beautiful women start comparing birth canal horror stories.

'I delivered the baby myself on the bathroom floor.'

'Did anyone eat the placenta?' I can't help asking. I don't know anyone who has apart from Hugh Fearnley-Whittingstall who cooked one on his series *TV Dinners*, which does make a change from oven chips and nuggets.

Here's an example of what is good about our post-industrial, soulless, non-sustainable modern society as opposed to tribal society. We don't have to eat our placentas. If we're low on vitamin B we can send our baby fathers out to buy a wholemeal tuna mayo sandwich and a jar of Marmite. Or better still, over to the Archway Tavern for a pint of Guinness.

Christophe is looking unusually pale, as if he might not want Hugh's recipe. 'I thought this was a surf club, shouldn't you be talking about surfing?'

Oh yes. He's right, but what have we got to talk about? We haven't any heroic, death-defying feats to compare – or maybe we have, maybe that's why we're talking about childbirth. We're convincing ourselves that we've done something more hard core, tougher and scarier than big-wave surfing.

We may have had a few *near*-surf experiences, but nothing that will get us through dessert. Most of us have been out surfing with our husbands or boyfriends at some point, and most of us have taken a long time to recover from the experience. I have a conspiracy theory about this now. I don't think those men were trying to teach us to surf at all. I think they were making sure their women stayed on the beach by proving that they were doing something deeply courageous and scary and practically impossible to learn. That's why they always took us out in waves that they claimed were less than a metre yet were clearly ten times that size, then disappeared over the horizon leaving us to get washed onto the rocks. That way we were happy to stay on the beach minding the kids and the cooler, waiting to massage sensual oils into their aching muscles when they got back on shore.

I don't really blame them. Surfing *is* deeply courageous and scary and practically impossible to learn, and I'd love to have someone waiting on the beach with a cold Corona and some ylang ylang oil. Once you've got a taste for riding the wild waves it's extremely hard to say, 'You go out when the conditions are perfect, I'll stay on the beach and babysit, and do the shopping and cooking.' It requires a spirit of selflessness that may be found more often in women than in men.

There probably are New Men out there who would wait on the beach for you, but the Pays Basque isn't the best place to start looking. Anyway, it's a catch-22 situation. If I did find a man willing to stay home to hoover the house and bake scones while I took the wild wave, I probably wouldn't fancy him anyway. The *vive la différence* mentality has got to me.

Seeing Christophe's distress we obligingly change the subject to sport. The training is working, I can now run like a guinea pig and do sit-ups like a guinea pig, and who knows, in time maybe I'll be able to surf like a guinea pig too. But as the conversation goes on, I begin to think that when the other women say 'unfit', they're using a different scale of reference. I begin to see a pattern forming.

'I haven't been running for *days*... '

'I did a bit of rock climbing in Spain last weekend... '

'When I was an aerobics teacher... '

'I went off-piste skiing when I was living with a mountain guide... '

'The second time I climbed Mount Kilimanjaro... '

'I used to ride all the time when I was going out with a rodeo cowboy... '

The last three are all from Taryn; no wonder she's bored of the school run.

'I used to swim for the county, my grandmother stopped me because she thought I'd never find a man if my shoulders got too big,' said Jo who is English, and I thought I could have counted on her to have stuck to things like three-legged beer races.

The other women are Spanish, Belgian, Swedish and Norwegian.

'I've been to Norway, which part are you from?' I'm trying to change the subject.

'Oh, you wouldn't know it. Hammerfest in Lapland, it's the northernmost town in the world.'

She's wrong; I've been to Hammerfest. After hitch-hiking round Iceland my friend Mo and I thought it would be a laugh to hitch to the northernmost town in the world, but it was a bit further than we thought; 2,000 km further, making Oslo further from Hammerfest than it is from Rome. By the time we got to Hammerfest we'd run out of money and needed to get back to London, so we had to turn back almost straight away. I only had enough time to buy a pair of reindeer-fur slippers from some old Lapps, have a couple of beers and kiss a handsome young Viking conscript who was posted on the Russian border.

'Really? What were you doing there? Yachting, Nordic skiing, ice climbing?'

'No, I went to the disco.'

BOOBS AND TUBES

We wait until the early summer for the first outdoor meeting of the surf club. It's a year since the dark hour when I thought I might have to give up the whole idea, but I'm optimistic after the training if still a little nervous of the monster billows. It's a bit like the first day at school except that we're on the beach, we're here to have fun and we're grown up and wearing bikinis. So, it's not at all like the first day of school, it's more like the first episode of a series about glamorous forty-something women in various stages of marriage/divorce/childcare: *Desperate Housewives* meets *Baywatch*.

While the others are running around doing beach press-ups, strapping on their leashes and generally looking as if they're involved in filming a scary fitness video, I pick one out instantly as having promising surf buddy potential. Taryn is wearing a black lace vintage dress and cowboy boots and is finding a shaded nook in the rock for her cooler.

'I know we were meant to bring cake, but I thought beer might be more useful.'

I love this woman already. It's not just the beer, it's the look of blank terror on her face that makes me think she could be a soul mate.

'We might need them later when we get out of the water, don't you think?'

'I think I need one now before I get in! Is Steve coming?'

'He should be here any minute,' she says, looking out to sea.

Her husband, a Californian surfer, arrives a few minutes later in a Hawaiian canoe, wearing board shorts and a cowboy hat and carrying a couple of bass he's caught on the way over.

'I've got dinner.' He looks around. 'Wow, I love it. The Boobs and Tubes Surf Club!'

We go every Saturday until the insanity of the summer holidays hits and France grinds to a standstill. Our kids sometimes come along for a laugh. We've watched their first steps, their dance routines, their school plays in awe and wonder. Now it's their turn to stand on the shore and gasp in amazement.

'Did you see that great wave?' I ask Nat.

'Which one?'

Which one? They obviously don't want me to get big-headed. 'The one where I got one foot and my knee onto the board. I almost stood up, for God's sake! I think I could have made it if I hadn't hit that poodle.'

At this point Jo comes gliding past, standing effortlessly on her board, smiling and waving.

'How long has she been surfing?'

'I don't know, I thought she said it was her first day.' Shit, I expected a bit of solidarity from her. Then again she is from West Wittering, the Malibu of the English south coast.

And she's not the only one. A lot of the women seem to achieve the standing up manoeuver that has eluded me month after month. Damn it, all those wasted years spent drinking in the Colony Room, going to discos in Lapland, wearing body paint and painting pictures. I should obviously have been swimming for the county, climbing Mount Kilimanjaro and dating rodeo cowboys.

Taryn's right, when I get out of the water I do need a beer. She opens the cooler.

'Eugh, sorry, Steve's put the fish in there. Do you mind fishy beer?'

'Don't worry, I think I've got enough seaweed down my cleavage to make a California roll. Pass the fish.'

There's something very heart-warming and inspiring about learning with other people who understand concepts like fear and waterproof mascara. We don't, like most surfers, bullshit about the size of waves; we tell it like it is: 'That was ginormous, magnificent, fucking massive, you're a total big-wave hero... '

Christophe may chip in with something like, 'It was only about thirty centimetres high,' but we're not fooled.

For a long time I prayed that the sea would be glassy calm for the weekly surf club rendezvous, and felt sick with fear if the waves got over what Christophe described as 50 centimetres although it looked at least five times that size to me. But I kept at it and I eventually stood up.

'I did it! Did you see that, kids? I stood up in one go! Wow, I think I deserve a beer for that!'

The kids look at each other, then at me.

'Mum, aren't you meant to be, you know... er... in the water, on your surfboard... '

I'm lying on the kitchen floor practising my take-off. If you can't jump to your feet on the beach – or in your bedroom or on your kitchen floor – you're unlikely to be able to do it on a moving surfboard out at sea.

'Baby steps, just getting my technique perfected on dry land.'

Less dangerous too. I have knocked over the garbage a couple of times, but no serious injuries.

ZEN AND THE ART OF SANDWICH MAKING

I'm in the local bar having another crisis about the state of my surfing.

'Why does it matter so much?' Patrique the owner asks me, very dapper in a pink ruffled shirt standing in front of a sequinned statue of Ganesh.

Learning to surf has a symbolic significance for me. It's not just that I'd really like to be out there walking on water, I've set it as a task, like in a fairy story. Go out there and stand on the wave and then you will have the key to the magical kingdom, but I warn you, if you fail, you will shrivel up and wither away and be destined to wear twin-sets and pearls and drink sweet sherry for the rest of your life. So now not learning to surf has become a symbol of complete failure, especially after a few of the knockout house rum punches.

'Maybe you need to do a bit of yoga. I'll take you to a class.'

It's one thing that should work in my favour actually, the fact that I've been doing yoga since I was eight. Although it's

113

not exactly a sport, all that bending must count for something even if the Zen-like calm that I must have acquired along the way seems to be buried pretty deep at the moment. I found a yoga book on my mother's shelf – the woman on the cover was a glamorous blonde in a lilac leotard, with full-on 1960s make up and back-combed hair. I suppose she became a bit of an early role model.

When I was bored and nagging my mother, 'What can I do? I'm BORED!' she'd either give me some paints or the yoga book, which I guess was less messy. I'd put on a bit of her Yardley's green eyeshadow and my ballet clothes and go to the bottom of the garden to sit in the Lotus position or stand on my head for a while.

I've never lost the habit; I still go and stand on my head when I'm at a loss, but not usually in ballet clothes.

I did some classes in Dingle. Our teacher was glamorous in a more earthy way, draped in brightly coloured ethnic prints and tie-dyes. She had five children and was understandably very into the relaxation side of yoga. The problem was that I would come home from a class feeling that I was at one with the world, covered in golden light and generally pretty airy-fairy, and I'd find it hard to adjust to the idea of cooking fish fingers, feeding the chickens, boiling up a box of crab claws and becoming an international art star. I just felt like basking in my rainbow-coloured aura and going into the garden to hug a tree. Except that there are no trees in Baile na nGall, so I'd have to hug a clump of pampas grass, but it's a bit sharp and I'd get all confused.

Then Alice would stand up in her high chair demanding baby mush and my husband would stand up in his demanding a ham salad sandwich, and I'd get all task-overloaded and irritable.

I was looking at the universe as a holistic entity, so how much mustard I put in the sandwich seemed of little significance.

'Aaaaagh, this is disgusting,' Nick chokes. 'You've put way too much mustard in it.'

'Do you really think it matters in the cosmic plan? Eat the sandwich and shut the fuck up.'

'Are you sure yoga calms you down?' he asks.

'Yes, why do you ask?' I yell and leave the room slamming the door behind me.

Patrique picks me up a few days later in a vintage Mercedes with a crucifix on the dashboard and a Hawaiian garland hung from the rear-view mirror, and takes me down to St-Jean-de-Luz to meet my new guru. He trained in India, he's totally Basque and completely charming. He's also wearing a pair of socks with 'Old Surfers Never Die' written on them.

Before the class starts we discuss smoking.

'I only smoke cigars after a good meal with a glass of cognac,' he says. One of the students seems a little surprised. 'You don't drink too, do you?'

'Why would I not drink? Of course I drink; I love wine. Everyone has a different path, a different destiny. Abstinence is not my path.'

Another time I arrive to find the women comparing recipes for foie gras; it may be a yoga class, but we're still in France. Tofu is not part of our destiny.

After the class the teacher asks me, 'Is there anything you didn't understand?'

'Well, maybe. What exactly did you mean when you say I must "cease to exist"?' I'm assuming he didn't mean it personally as we seemed to get on pretty well. Maybe it's a language thing.

'Haha! Yes, poor Wilma, she comes to one class and I tell her to cease to exist. Maybe you should start with something easier, like relaxing your tongue.'

He's right; that is a lot easier.

'But the point is you have to erase your ego to discover true enlightenment.'

I don't know, maybe we could discuss this over some foie gras, a glass of Sauternes and a Cuban cigar? This is a bit of a problem for me. I don't feel as if I need my ego erased. On the contrary, my ego needs artificial resuscitation.

In another attempt to calm down and become a little more Zen, I go for a massage. Afterwards I'm feeling pleasantly oily and relaxed, and then my masseuse says, 'I'd really like you to come over for a hypnotherapy session next time.'

She tells me that it's a great way to relieve stress and it will be good for my creativity. She's planning to hypnotise me and then put lots of positive, calm thoughts in my head, which will stay with me deep down but resurface without my even knowing while I'm painting.

I feel my brow wrinkling. My tongue is not relaxed.

'Sorry, didn't you understand?' She's explaining the idea in French.

Yes, I did, but I'm thinking how awful that could be. I'll be in the middle of a dark, meaningful, mildly fucked-up painting and suddenly happy positive thoughts will come bubbling to the surface. I'll start painting rainbows, seagulls in the sunset and dolphins frolicking in the surf. I realise that calming down may be counter-productive and explain that I have to maintain my stress levels.

I keep going to the yoga class despite having issues with erasing my ego. And I do try. I am told I must want nothing, desire nothing and expect nothing. I breathe in and out; I imagine white light all around me; it makes me feel good. But somewhere inside me there's a little voice saying, 'I want it all and I want it now.'

It does strike me that the classes give me insight into ordering a beer at Patrique's bar, Heteroclito, which is notoriously difficult. It's my favourite bar but I often take the precaution of having a drink before I go. But now I have insight into the yogic philosophy behind the bar, which might help.

OK, let's try it. I'm sitting in Heteroclito on my bar stool. I don't want or desire anything. I don't expect anything, but if a beer were part of my destiny I would accept it. Oh damn. I'm dying of thirst. I'd love a plate of marinated tuna and that new barman's pretty gorgeous. Not good. Let's try again. I neither want nor need a beer, but I will be open to one if it comes my way. Patrique comes over, 'Here you go, Wilma, a large beer on the house.' Erasing ego worked, although I have to stifle a giggle at the French concept of a large beer.

The French may be the best chefs and lovers in the world, but they're rubbish at drinking beer. A large beer is a *demi*, 250 centilitres, which is about half a pint and I really get the piss taken out of me for ordering it. Most women go for a *bock*, which translates in English as 'a sip', 125 centilitres that barely covers the bottom of the glass. I try telling them that a Baile na nGall fisherman could get through 40 *'bocks'* for breakfast before going out and catching that gravlax they're serving, but it makes no difference.

Well I've learned to order beer using my new Zen techniques, maybe I can apply them to the equally important task of learning to surf.

I'm a bit surprised at my yoga class when my guru tells me I've put on weight and that I 'owe it to myself as a woman to have abs'.

As far as I know, going back to the Buddha himself, a six pack wasn't the first requirement of yogic practice.

'Lose your ego and slim down' wasn't the advice I was hoping to get from my guru. Maybe like the French attitude to beer, the French attitude to yoga is something I'll have to get used to.

I've always thought, deep down, that it wasn't in my destiny to have abs. But then again I always thought it wasn't in my destiny to be a surfer, and I'm beginning to think the two may be quite closely connected.

In the end I need mind and body – maybe I owe it to myself as a *surfer* to have abs.

I decide to take what I need from the class, as he told me. I'm not ready to lose my ego, but I am ready to do some sit-ups, relax my tongue and accept his philosophy that you should 'Live each moment as if it was the first and last moment of your life.'

Eventually something works; whether it's the yogic breathing or the press-ups, I couldn't say. It's the old mind or body argument.

HAPPY TODDLER

The kids can laugh all they want at my practice baby steps in the kitchen – and they do – but having perfected the technique on dry land, the day finally comes when I manage it in the water. We meet at Olatua but the waves are way too big. We head down the coast to another beach where the waves are small; in fact you have to get out the binoculars to see them from the promenade, but what the hell, it's a wide beach.

We're on the Spanish border. You can see an old church in Fuenterrabía across the sand dunes and the music from a fiesta drifts across the river. It could be the set of a spaghetti western except for the statuesque Spanish women walking along the water's edge in flowery, old-fashioned swimsuits and flowery, plastic swimming hats.

I stand up! I'm sure someone pushed me in to the wave, but no one helped me to my feet. That's it, my ambition achieved, maybe I should just stop now while the going is good. I could avoid any more injuries or humiliation and just say that I learned to stand on a surfboard. That was my goal and I did it. But – if you're that kind of person, a something-to-prove

Piscean with an addictive personality – once you've got to your feet, you're hooked.

Of course, I didn't stay standing long – about half a second real time – and I wasn't miraculously able to surf after that, but it was a turning point. There were days it felt as if someone had oiled my board or I'd drunk a few margaritas before I got in the water... or on bad days, both. But as the summer progressed I got to the stage where I just occasionally wished the waves were a little bigger rather than smaller. The recurring dream about tidal waves was replaced by a nightmare that I was wandering along a beach in a wetsuit with my board, but I couldn't find a wave. I found out that it's even more exciting surfing when you can do it and a lot less exhausting, I sometimes even came home with no bruises at all!

But that first time, at that magical moment, I was the best surfer in the world, screaming the primal scream you'll hear on beaches around the world when someone gets to their feet for the first time: 'Yeeeeeessssss, I am walking on water.'

That night there's a party on the beach. I'm like a happy toddler if you can imagine a toddler drinking Mexican beer and margaritas. I'm so excited I have to tell anyone willing to listen the incredible story of the time I stood up on a surfboard. I can't shut up about it. I see a friend making that be-quiet-quickly-before-you-embarrass-yourself-any-more face behind my captive audience.

Who am I talking to? Oh, it's Martin Potter, who was world champion in 1989. He's the only British surfer to have won the world title. He was brought up in South Africa, but the national papers were so proud they behaved as if he'd done his training on the River Thames. Am I expecting him to be impressed? An image of him surfing Pipeline in Hawaii flashes into my head. I freeze halfway through the bit where I trip over the leash and do a face plant into the sand, but surfers are generous about this kind of thing. Everyone remembers the first time they stood up, even if they *were* only five.

'Good for you, Wilma, have another beer.'

Standing up also, in a strange way, helps with my painting. Of course you have to weigh this up against the amount of studio time I've sacrificed to get to this stage, but I try to take surf time from other less important parts of my busy schedule, like baking cakes, cleaning the house, socialising or lying on the beach.

I've started some large collages of women surfing and I feel I would be living a lie if I finished them before I could stand up. If I had never managed to stand up I would have left them unfinished as a reminder of my failure. 'All painting is autobiographical,' as Picasso said, and mine is very obviously full of self-portraits and stories from my life. The surf queens are part of a new series of paintings inspired by iconic images of women that I've loved since I was a child. Some are taken from flamenco postcards, vintage hula girl beer mats or circus posters. Then there are carnival queens from old copies of *National Geographic*, from parades in San Sebastián and fragmented memories of a wild week I spent at Veracruz Mardi Gras many years ago. I don't feel the need to get out my grass skirt or my castanets, tame lions or sit on a float in a feather headdress and fishnet tights, but it is a point of pride not to finish the *Surfeuses et Sirènes* (Surf Chicks and Mermaids) series until I have clambered to my feet.

Making the collages is quite ritualistic. Every morning I go beachcombing with my beloved Bibi. She picks up old fish heads and seagull guano; I pick up fishing lures, silk roses, Spanish brandy bottles, mermaid's purses, doll's limbs and other worthless bits of treasure washed up to the high tide line. Anything and everything goes onto the collages along with these *objets trouvés*: gold leaf, sequins, beads, dried flowers and peacock feathers; flamenco postcards and plastic doilies from Spain; postage stamps from Outer Mongolia and Western Sahara; a paper bag from a fish and chip shop in Brighton; a parasol from a rum punch I drank in Guadalupe.

One day Alice catches me gluing the clippings of her fringe to *Surfeuse en Rose*.

'*Oh là là!* The world will hear about this when you're famous, how my mother stole my hair for her paintings.' A story for the *Mommie Dearest* memoirs.

'You weren't going to keep it, were you? Think of it as payment for the hair cut.' But my kids drive a hard bargain; I end up offering her 10 per cent of the painting's selling price.

The collages become like offerings. Everything I stick on them has a special significance: 24-carat gold leaf for wealth; dried shamrocks and Candomblé ribbons from Bahia for luck; sequins for fame; and rubbish from the beach to keep me grounded. I rescue attractive food wrappers from friends' bins and drink litres of Tahitian beer to make a frame from the empty cans. Yes, it's a tough life.

When I show the paintings at an exhibition called *Mardi Gras* in London, everyone likes the one of a woman doing the splits on her surfboard best.

'Wow, can you do that?'

Do you ever feel as if people are expecting too much from you?

Part
Three

THE MAMAS
SURF CLUB

We do consider keeping the Boobs and Tubes name as a joke, but Christophe isn't convinced.

'I see the boobs, but where are the tubes? I'm honestly not sure that you'll ever surf tubes... ' A tube being a wave that closes over your head, but is so big and hollow you can stand up inside it. The idea is to glide through the tube and come out the other end, shaking your fists in the air in triumph. I get his point.

The name has to work in French and English, although at this point Florence is the only French woman in the club. This is not because we're xenophobic ex-pats sticking together. It's the reason we started the club in first place – very few French women surf.

By the next year we have quite a few, but in the beginning it's very women of the world. Patrique from the bar, which is now our official clubhouse, suggests Shakti Surf Club. Shakti being the great goddess in Hindu religion; a manifestation of feminine creative power and primordial cosmic energy, according to Wikipedia. I rather like that although my performance in the water to date might not live up to the name.

'Isn't that something to do with tantric sex?' one woman asks, so we decide against it in case others think similarly and we'll have even more to live up to. On the other hand we want to avoid sounding too mumsy and middle aged.

'How about the Nanas Surf Club?' Christophe suggests. *Nana* means attractive woman or a hot chick in French, although the word has been slightly ruined for me as it's the most popular brand of sanitary towels. Jo and I explain that 'nana' is a granny in English, and we're definitely not that old.

'OK, what about Mamas?'

We check that one in the slang dictionary. Definition: a sexually attractive, usually mature woman.

That's it, the perfect mix of mums and red-hot mamas. The Mamas Surf Club is official.

I come up with the heartfelt motto: Out of the kitchen and into the surf.

We continue meeting up on Saturdays. Everyone can stand up now – some for longer than others. The fearless Jo and Florence are getting good, and Johanna looks as if she's been surfing forever and is training for her instructor's exam already.

I end up with three main surf buddies: Florence, Jo and Taryn.

Florence and I met outside the primary school when I first arrived, and my Alice and her daughter are best friends, so we're already close.

Jo arrived in the village six months ago with her husband and two of her four sons. At first we avoided each other, sick of being told, 'There's another English family in the village, you should get together,' as if we were desperate to drink gin and tonic and play bridge with ex-pats. If we wanted to meet other Brits we could have stayed in the UK, but once we meet we get over our prejudice. Our children are at school together and her son Tom and Daisy form the English rebel contingent. They go busking together in St-Jean-de-Luz: Tom playing guitar and Daisy singing, which convinces the school that English kids are '*très* rock and roll'. Jo and I quite often have a gin and tonic together when we come out of the water, so maybe there's something in the ex-pat cliché, although we talk about surf moves not bridge moves.

Taryn and I definitely bonded in fear and enthusiasm for the après-surf beer.

She is in some ways the most like me except that she's from Idaho, used to ride a horse to school, has dated rodeo cowboys and occasionally chews tobacco, which all sound very exotic to me. Maybe we're not that alike after all, but she's also an artist, not professional, and a traveller, our kids are the same age and so are we.

The difference between us is that Taryn is pretty sporty: she's skied all her life, dated a mountain guide and trekked in the Himalayas and shot the rapids in Montana, she jogs and does yoga, but has hardly ever been in the ocean.

My sporting history may be brief, but I have spent hours, days, weeks of my life in the sea, pools, lakes, rivers, anywhere it's wet. Maybe it's being a Piscean – if there's water I have a natural urge to douse myself in it. You can rely on me to jump in the pool naked at a party, go skinny dipping at midnight and swim in the freezing English Channel or Blasket Sound on New Year's Day.

What Taryn and I do share is a primal fear of waves. Waves are dangerous, we are programmed to avoid them. All my life I've been warned about rip tides and now I'm meant to search them out and deliberately put myself in their path in order to be swept out to where the really big waves are breaking.

Taryn and I may not be the most natural surfers in the club, but we do have obsession on our side. Perhaps it's the determination to conquer our fear and the fact that we're the oldest in the group that keeps us going: Taryn is a few months older than me. Being the oldest surf bunnies in town is a dubious accolade, so we have something to prove.

We try never to miss a session, but once back on land after a couple of hours in the water, I fall asleep wherever I sit down and dream of tidal waves as soon as my eyes close.

None of the Mamas have graduated to surfing alone yet, so if we miss a lesson there's a whole week to wait.

The weather in Biarritz fluctuates between tropical paradise and Bay of Biscay sea shanty. The thing about meeting at a given time every Saturday is that we have to surf whatever the weather throws at us: taking the imperfect wave can be good training, but there are limits.

One stormy Saturday I ring Taryn.

'I'm not going whatever Johanna says to persuade me,' I tell Taryn. 'Have you seen the colour of the water?'

It's been raining all week, there have been floods in the Pyrenees and the water is a sinister yellow ochre colour. It looks like chicken soup and is full of broken trees, dead fish and farm run off. I've just found a nice wooden chair washed up on the beach and brought it home thinking it will suit the distressed decor. (Nat isn't impressed, 'What are you – a tramp?' Nat's going through a teenage phase of craving normality and wishing I'd buy my furniture at Ikea.)

'I'm not going either,' says Taryn, whose son Hayden found a dead goat on the beach.

But as club session time approaches I begin to crack and all Johanna has to say is: 'Come on, don't be a wimp!'

I call Taryn back.

'You know, I'm thinking it's so wet anyway, we might as well put on our wetsuits and enjoy it. After all what are we going to do if we *don't* surf?'

'My beach bag's already packed,' says Taryn.

The Mamas' Perfect Wave is different to the widely accepted notion of the Perfect Wave. When the Mamas find a Perfect Wave, we drive on to look for something quarter the size. Small and perfectly formed is ideal, otherwise, just small will do. 'Never too small for the Mamas' is another of our mottoes for a while. As the Basque coast curves down from Biarritz to Spain, with surf beaches all the way, the waves generally get smaller and more mellow the further south you go. If the swell is too big we head to Hendaye on the border. Cruising along the coast in Christophe's camouflage surf bus is one of the perks of the Mamas Surf Club meetings for me. I sometimes wish we could just stay in the bus chatting. On the way to the break we talk about what our kids are up to, relationships and stuff. Alarmingly four of the original Mamas are either getting divorced or about to. I'm not sure whether this means surfing is bad for your marriage or that divorced women are more likely to surf.

On the way home after the session, we move on to more important topics like how to angle the board, duckdiving and how to stay Zen in a big set.

Christophe's son Bruno often comes with us: he's a ten-year-old competition surfer who's been surfing since he could walk, a 'grom' in surf talk. He paddles around us, giving us the benefit of his superior wisdom and chooses one Mama for the 'Wave of the Week' award at the end of the afternoon. I remember the day I won it with great pride and as the pinnacle of my sporting achievements to date.

We try bringing our own kids to the sessions, but it spoils the illusion of the Mamas being a bunch of carefree teenagers. We're meant to be getting away from our responsibilities one afternoon a week not bringing them out into the water with us where we're expected to react in a caring and adult fashion when they paddle over to say 'I'm cold and tired and hungry,' and resist the temptation to answer, 'So what? I'm just getting the hang of the take-off.'

Apart from maternal duty there's the added stress of not running into or over your friend's children in the water. We laugh it off when we crash into each other, but sending another Mama's ten-year-old back to the beach crying and covered in bruises is somehow deeply uncool. Women's killer instincts come out when their children are threatened and the Mamas don't want to lose the surf sister vibe, so in the end we get another instructor and another van for our beloved offspring and subtly suggest they go to a different beach.

Après-surf depends on the weather too. If it's cold and rainy we eat chocolate and bags of churros – greasy Spanish doughnuts – washed down with Thermoses of tea in the bus. If it is warm and sunny we sit outside Heteroclito drinking cold beer, eating Guernika chillies and watching the sun set while we tell our epic wave stories to anyone willing to listen.

The last session of the summer has gone down in history as Big Saturday.

We arrive at our favourite beach in Bidart to find the waves are off the scale for the Mamas.

What we would normally do is pile straight back in the bus and drive south. The problem is that we've arranged a barbecue and carried coolers full of fine viands, beer and rosé down the cliff in the 40-degree-Celsius heat. Despite the 'Out of the kitchen and into the surf' motto, I had even prepared a salsa and an artistic salad of purple potatoes, green beans and yellow tomatoes. The surf papas, children and assorted groupies are arriving later to light the fires and cook. So even off-the-scale waves could not make us consider walking away from the surf – or the coolers.

If the surf looked massive from the car park, it looked like the north shore of Hawaii as we walked down to the beach, parallel lines of swell stretching out to the horizon, stripes of turquoise, cobalt, indigo and ultramarine: a cosmic colour chart. The sight that surfers dream of strikes fear into the hearts of craven Surf Mamas like myself. I wasn't ready for the Perfect Wave.

It looked like a photo from a surf mag, the kind of photo that would tempt you to buy an under-sized over-priced bikini. Or really, much more like an ad for board shorts. In the surf media, men are depicted as hard core and full of attitude, surfing the wild wave, standing on beaches with sexy Brazilian women in thongs. An idealised lifestyle that men around the world might aspire to. I aspire to it myself.

Women on the other hand are usually depicted jumping around on beaches waving their arms in the air like cheerleaders, playing volleyball with an invisible net and ball or striking sexy poses on towels without a wave in sight.

The psychology behind the marketing is that men dream of surfing monster waves, and women prefer to lie on the beach waiting for the guy on the monster wave to come in and buy them a glass of rosé.

It makes sense in a way: 99 per cent of women want to look hot in a bikini, whereas only one per cent want to ride monster waves.

I am part of the one per cent, heat stroke having melted my grey matter.

As soon as I get out on the water I realise my mistake: I see the logic about five minutes too late. I'd give quite a lot at this moment to be jumping around the beach in an over-priced under-sized bikini or sitting on a towel in a sexy pose waiting for a demigod with attitude to come in and buy me a glass of rosé. Hell, I wouldn't even have to wait for the dude, I have a cooler full of rosé of my own on the beach. The only question is how to get back to it without any collateral damage to my body or my beloved surfboard.

It would make so much more sense to be looking at a photo of this wave in a sexist surf mag than waiting for it to break over my head. I shouldn't just be waiting of course; I should be preparing a move called an Eskimo roll. (Surfers are nowhere near politically correct enough to re-christen it the Inuit roll.) An Eskimo roll might sound like a dessert – a cross between Swiss roll and baked Alaska with a side order of seal blubber – but it's not, it's where you flip your board over and try to swim through the wave upside down and backwards without letting go of the board. The roll is about as much fun as it sounds. Its purpose is to get you out through the breaking waves, avoiding surfing backwards onto the beach (very embarrassing) or chucking the board behind you and knocking out one of your new best friends (bad surf etiquette for obvious reasons). Whether your Eskimo roll works or not, you have to be seen to be trying.

I know it will be futile – the result will be the same if I do it or not. My board will be dragged from my hands by the force of the wave, I will be dragged after it, washed in to the impact zone, spat out in the shore break and then forced to start all over again by my over-enthusiastic surf coach.

Built into this is the idea that I might actually *want* to get out again, way out to beyond where the waves are breaking, and catch one just as it rears up into a solid wall of deep green water and foam begins to blow off the top. In theory this is what I want, but my gut feeling is that I might die out there. My heart is pounding like a stoned surf bum playing the bongo drums, my hands are shaking and I feel dizzy with fear... and excitement, which is what keeps me out here I suppose.

There's no point my coach telling me it's only 1.5 metres. It offers no comfort.

If you find yourself in this situation, remember that 1.5 metres is the height at the *back* of the wave; the part you surf, the face, can be twice that height, so we're talking about room-height walls of water.

Battling waves is an enjoyable way to spend the afternoon, but after a while the novelty wears off and I go back to the beach, not looking much like a bikini model at all. I am waterlogged and sandblasted, I have a thick lip and fish net in my hair. Now, where is that hunky dude in board shorts waiting to buy me a glass of rosé, or doesn't it work this way round?

I decide that discretion is the better part of valour and hang out in the white wash pretending I'm trying to catch waves and waiting for a reasonable moment to get back to dry land and crack open a beer.

The only one of us who didn't seem to be freaking out was Florence who has a reputation for not knowing the meaning of the word fear, and also has a really annoying habit of keeping her hair perfectly coiffed in a wipeout. I've checked over and over again – most of us come out of the water looking dishevelled at best. I look like I have a clump of wet seaweed attached to my head, but Florence manages to look as if she'd visited an underwater hair salon.

Flo has mastered the Eskimo roll and got way out past the bar. We watch in amazement as she takes off on a mountainous 2-metre wave. There's general euphoria, a chorus of '*Oh là là!*' and 'Oh my fucking God!' as she charges down the wall of water. No one sees what happens next, but when she comes in to a hero's welcome she's a bit shell-shocked. The glorious moment was apparently more fun for the spectators than the hero of the hour. After she disappeared from view in the foam she broke her leash and hit her head on the sandbar.

But it's a proud moment for the Mamas watching from the safety of the shallows and we've never let Florence forget it.

When we get to the barbecue we find that some of the men are not adapting well to their status as Surf Widows. Lighting barbecues under the blazing sun and being so close to perfect waves they can't catch isn't making things any easier, and some of them look as if they're about to prove the theory of spontaneous combustion. It's hard to know how to be diplomatic.

'Oh turn that sausage over it looks a bit burnt and open another beer for me, I'm just going back to check the swell.'

I don't have an overheated man to placate, so I grab a beer and go back down to the beach. As I stand there at sunset looking at the waves I've almost surfed, I realise there's been a slight shift in my mindset. I may be feeling bruised and battered, but I'm no longer thinking of the waves as my worst nightmare, I'm dreaming of the day I will surf them.

ALPHA FEMALE

I'm beginning to wonder if it's time to look for a man to light my fire and open my beers. Although having been married for a very, very long time I like being single, in fact I think I'm developing a commitment phobia. My sister picked up on this when we were talking on the phone.

'You know, Wilma, you don't have to wash their socks on the first date,' she sighed.

It can be hard being single in the most romantic country in the world as I found out last Valentine's Day. The French invented lingerie, champagne, Chanel Nᵒ. 5, French kissing and Paris. Think of all the words we take from their language: *rendez-vous, femme fatale, ménage à trois, décolleté, déshabillé, soixante-neuf*. And what do we give back? Le parking, le shopping, le hamburger, le sandwich.

I've never enjoyed Valentine's Day much. My ex-husband was pretty good at bringing home romantic gifts: bunches of flowers, champagne, perfume, live lobsters and stuff like that, but rarely on 14 February. He was a fully signed-up member of the Hallmark cards conspiracy theory, and had no truck with

Valentine's Day as the feast day of an ancient Christian martyr (whose last words were, apparently: 'Keep the faith, overcome the heathen masses and always buy your lady friends a box of Milk Tray on my birthday'). Personally I think Valentine's Day was invented by Galeries Lafayette to unload winter season's underwear at the end of January.

So, I have two issues with Valentine's Day this year. Firstly, I have to buy my own French knickers, and secondly French lingerie shops don't stock my size.

There was a moment when I thought I had shrunk to the size where I would finally be able to hit the lingerie sales, but it was a dream turns nightmare scenario. I was reminiscing about it the other day with Daisy.

'Do you remember when you shrivelled up like a little raisin?' she asked.

My weight has fluctuated between size ten and size 16 over the years. At size 16 expressions like statuesque, curvaceous and Rubenesque were used a little too often for my liking. Rubens' women are gorgeous, but you can't really imagine one of them surfing, can you?

On the other hand, I haven't been too thin since I was 11 when the school doctor told my mother to make me drink a glass of cod liver oil twice a week. This traumatic experience put me off striving for size zero and drinking fish guts forever.

But at one point in my training I lose so much weight I can take off my jeans without undoing them. This is due not only to taking up sport suddenly at an advanced age, but to post-separation stress syndrome – a side effect of divorce – and waning enthusiasm for hanging out in the kitchen.

Maybe I've been brainwashed into believing that a woman can never be too rich or too thin. At first I enjoy the novelty and look forward to buying a bikini that fits me and joining the ladies who don't lunch on the sand without feeling like the token plus-size model at the *Vogue* Christmas party.

I don't see how much weight I have lost until I go into a shop and ask for a pair of size 30 jeans.

'Who for?' the assistant asks me, looking genuinely confused.

'Oh, do you think a size twenty-nine might fit me? I've lost a bit of weight recently.'

She comes back with a size 26 and it fits. Wow! Some tiny little part of me screams: 'I'm a skinny girl at last!' But the shop assistant won't let me buy the jeans because they look so awful.

I feel like Alice in *Alice in Wonderland*. I wanted to shrink and get into the magical world of thin people, but now I'm too small and I look crap. Women are telling me to put on weight, men are telling me to put on weight, my children are telling me to put on weight.

I pass on the cod liver oil and instead go to the Irish shop in Bayonne and buy enough Guinness – full of iron, B vitamins and bum-enhancing calories – to fill my fridge.

A surf Mecca might sound like the ideal place to be a single woman, but it has its bad points as well as its good ones.

On the good side, you're surrounded by bronzed surf gods. The thing about surfing is you naturally get a tan, and if you're not fit, you might sink. Black neoprene is very 007, and wet hair covers a multitude of coiffure crimes.

Then there's that cool surfie style. A surfer would rather go naked than wear Speedos, as you will notice walking through any parking lot on the Côte Basque. As an artist, a naturist and a woman, I have no complaints about hanging out in car parks being surrounded by board-short models stripped down to their Maori tattoos. There's also the swashbuckling piratical mentality that makes men want to sit out in a wild ocean on a Sunday afternoon instead of hanging out at a golf club or in a tool shed.

But it's all a bit of an illusion; the men are only single in the water. Back on the beach it's like an audition for the Pirelli calendar: women running across the hot sand in bikinis, their hair blowing in the breeze, carrying warm towels and cold beers.

'Good session, *chéri?*'

I look around to see if any men are running slow motion across the sand or waiting decoratively on beach towels to congratulate their girlfriends. No luck.

When you're in your forties you don't 'date' apparently. You do something more mature and considered called recoupling or repartnering. When you've had kids and gone through marriage and divorce, the simplicity of being a footloose and fancy-free twenty-something is a distant memory. Most of us forty-somethings come with baggage. I come with excess baggage. I've got three children, Russian hamsters, cockatiels, dwarf rabbits, Siamese fighting fish and a psychotically jealous sheepdog who can smell testosterone at 50 metres. I've got a surfboard and an addictive seawater habit that cannot be cured or interfered with making my repartnering options even more complex. For example, I might bore someone who didn't surf with my crest-of-a-wave stories, shipping forecasts and tidal coefficients. If I find a man who surfs better than me, I'll end up trailing 10 metres behind him in the water like every surf couple I've ever seen, and he'll yell, 'Paddle, paddle, paddle *chérie*,' across the line-up. I know this because men can't resist. Sometimes men I'm not even sleeping with do it to me.

On the other hand if I date a man who's worse at surfing than me, he will be an embarrassment in the water.

The idea of recoupling is that you view the person holistically: comparing age and compatibility of children, checking their children's school reports to see if they'll be a good influence and taking the dogs on play dates.

It's all very complicated and if you're worried about what a potential new boyfriend will think of your kids, it's not nearly as worrying as what your kids will think of your potential new boyfriend. I've been given all sorts of vetoes ranging from: 'You can't go out with him, his son brought a whole packet of sweets to school and didn't give me one!' to 'He wears high-waisted trousers.'

I wouldn't listen to these protests if *l'amour fou* struck, but the truth is I wouldn't go for a man who wore high waists or was stingy with his *bonbons*.

I'm looking for a man my age, or roughly my age – definitely over half my age unless he's very mature. I'm not sure what an acceptable age is actually. Over 30? Over 40? Over half my age? Over the age of consent?

But there's a catch 22: conventional wisdom says that I should be looking for a man with children of his own; a man with children might understand why you would spend an entire weekend setting up a table football set – he might even come round with his electric screwdriver and help. That's no problem, but am I meant to help put his children's football table together? I'd have to think twice about that. Anything involving nappies is out, and just thinking about other people's toddlers makes a little dark thundercloud form above my head. As for other people's teenagers...

So how does it work? Either I find a man with no kids, in which case why would he want mine? Or, worse still, a man with kids and why would I want his?

I met a man in London recently. He was gorgeous and we seemed to be hitting it off, then somehow the subject came up.

'Oh, you've got a kid?' He smiled and handed me a glass of wine.

'Three, actually.' Damn. The look on his face changes. Is the wine corked, honey? I don't know whether to laugh or cry or lie. I'm joking. I didn't mean it. They'll be leaving home soon. I could send them to boarding school. They're in France, for God's sake!

But the moment has passed.

The problem is that other people's children are not the same as your own. Your own children are the most beautiful, intelligent creatures on earth, unusually gifted and endlessly fascinating. The contents of their nappies could be displayed in art galleries. You'd defend them to the death and forgive them anything.

Daisy decided to put the forgiveness thing to the test one day; it followed something they'd been discussing at school.

'Mum, would you still love me if I committed murder?'

I'm not concentrating 100 per cent, I'm reading Nietzsche or waxing my board or something. I miss the obvious correct answer.

'No.'

'*What?*'

'Er, sorry, I mean I'm not sure, honey. It would probably depend on the nature of the murder.'

'*What?!!*'

I've missed my cue again.

'Well, crime of passion, yes, I guess so but some mindless racist murder, for example, I'd find harder to forgive.'

'I can't believe this! *All* my friends' mothers said they'd still love them when they were asked the question.'

Hang on, when did I get to be the bad guy? I'm not the one planning to hit the streets of St-Jean-de-Luz with an AK47. The idea of Daisy's glamorous 16-year-old friends going off on a killing spree in their retro dresses, Guess jeans and Brigitte Bardot make up makes me laugh.

'Why are you laughing? This is *appalling*. I don't have your unconditional love.'

Of course she does, but other people's children don't: most of them don't even have my conditional love. Maybe they could earn it if they were really cute, undemanding and gave me very nice Christmas presents. I don't mind other people's children coming round to play computer games and eat cookies now and then; I'll even take them to the cinema or bowling once a year. But I certainly don't want to have to help them with their irregular verbs or forgive them for murder.

It turns out that the recoupling situation is even more complicated than I thought. I open the paper and find an article about alpha females. The good-looking career woman in the photo is called Bibi, the same name as my dog. My dog wants to be an alpha female too, and she has a refreshingly straightforward approach to life: she snarls a bit, knocks the other bitch to the ground and sits on her.

What Bibi doesn't have to worry about while I do, according to this article, is the fact that alpha females have problems finding husbands. Intelligence just isn't an attractive trait in a woman. A woman's chances of getting married improve by 20 per cent with a 15-point drop in her IQ. (On the other hand, it could be that smart women are just too smart to get married.)

I might be really attractive in France as my IQ drops dramatically once I open my mouth and try to speak the language. But why am I assuming that I'm an alpha female in the first place? Does reading the article make me intelligent? Or the fact that I've managed to get hold of a copy of *The Guardian*? If I really was alpha I'd be able to read a French newspaper by now.

I look around me for evidence of alpha-ness. I have no furniture and there's nothing in the fridge but a piece of wild boar and a tin of tonic. I'm clever enough to have half a bottle of gin in the cupboard and a tray of ice in the freezer, but that doesn't make me Einstein. I don't have a super-high-powered job threatening to a man's ego, do I? Perhaps I can't afford to drop any IQ points after all.

If I can walk the fine line between being too stupid to pick up a Frenchman and too intelligent to pick up a Frenchman, it will do wonders for my language skills. It's common knowledge that the only place to get to grips with the subjunctive is in bed, though a Frenchman may also expect me to know how to cook foie gras, wear sexy underwear and drink beer out of a thimble. So for the meantime I've got myself a book called *Applied French Grammar*. I'm thinking of it as the low-maintenance option.

Would you rather go to the cinema or the theatre?

Do you prefer this dress or the one I wore last night?

Is it better to kill or to die?

What? This last one leaves me wondering: is it better to sit around reading grammar books or go to the bar and pick up the first well-spoken French surfer I see? Although with those textbook chat-up lines I might have to take a tip from Bibi and knock him to the ground and sit on him.

WOULD YOU LIKE
TO SEE MY BUST?

Having thought through the theory of recoupling and considered the pros and cons, I promptly forgot it all and picked up a young Californian surf dude.

I suppose I was over-excited about having learned to stand up on the board and thought I could do anything. But you have to know your limitations, and becoming a full-on surf chick was a step too far. But it seemed like destiny when I met the embodiment of my teenage dreams at a surf contest. He was auctioning a plaster cast of my breasts for charity. It seemed like a sign, but maybe I misread it.

The surf world didn't start off as the macho man's world it is today. In olde Hawaii, men and women surfed together in harmony and slept with each other every time they shared a wave (if you believe the rather over-used offshore chat-up line). Then Christian missionaries came along and warned the women of an eternity of hellfire and damnation that awaited unless they covered up and got back into the kitchen. The difficulty of paddling out in a Victorian bathing suit was also a turn-off. (It wasn't just the women who were forced to cover up – the missionaries almost managed to stamp out the 'ungodly' practice of surfing altogether at the end of the nineteenth century by banning the wearing of loincloths.)

There are a few early heroines of the surf; one of my favourites is the demigoddess Mamala, a mythical big-wave rider who could shape shift into the form of a giant lizard or shark. But that was then and this is now, and these days it's more important for women surfers to be able to shape shift into bikini models.

There's a bit of a fight on the competition circuit about this issue. Should a female athlete have to get silicon breast implants to keep her sponsors? Would she even be allowed to compete, let alone get sponsored, if she grew her armpit hair?

I don't have to worry too much about it as I'm unlikely to get sponsored by a surfwear company because their bikinis shape shift themselves down to my ankles in the changing room and I'm three times the age of their target market.

I suggested a new range to one of the bosses of a major women's surfwear company at a party one night: clothes that a woman could wear straight from the beach to the Ryanair VIP lounge in Biarritz airport and on to a book launch in London. They would be easy on, easy off for when hands and fingers go numb in the winter and perfect for the 50-year-old female surf bum.

'Great, Wilma,' she said. 'One problem – you'd be the only customer.'

Being on crutches and drinking schnapps when I made my pitch might not have helped.

I've been warned to stay away from the Roxy Jam – a women-only surf contest with bonus hula dancing, yoga sessions and girl band concerts – by a journalist friend who has covered it in the past.

'You know how most surf contests are a big ego boost,' she said, 'this is the opposite. A tent full of young beautiful surf chicks; it will totally destroy your ego.'

I haven't been to many yoga classes recently; the Roxy Jam could be a good way of getting rid of my ego and picking up a few style tips and free drinks while I discover the path to true enlightenment.

I've come to the organiser's tent to collect a bust for the Keep A Breast auction, which is raising money for breast cancer by selling plaster casts of surfers' breasts that have been decorated by artists. The blank white busts are hanging above the bar to dry, and a couple of guys are standing beneath them drinking beer and discussing which have been silicon enhanced.

'You can take whichever ones you want except Lisa Andersen's. They're reserved,' says the girl behind the desk, pointing to the world champion's perfect curves.

I think I would have found it intimidating to have the bust of the best woman surfer in the world hanging up in my studio anyway.

'Unless you want to cast your own?' the girl suggests.

As a founder of the Neo Naturists how could I resist? I'm all in favour of getting naked for charity: it's nice to know that you've stripped off for a good cause, not for something frivolous like an all-over tan or a piece of performance art.

I go to the back of the tent to do the cast and leave it to dry. When I come back the following day to collect my breasts, they've disappeared.

'I'm so sorry. One of the other artists came in and just loved them. He took them before we could stop him.' I'm quite flattered; I wish I'd had the presence of mind to ask for his phone number.

I take another pair off the shelf and stare at them for a while waiting for inspiration, which comes when I remember something that happened at one of my private views in London. My friend Alex Binnie is a tattoo artist and he wanted a painting; I wanted Mexican roses and day-of-the-dead skulls tattooed all over my chest. After four margaritas it seemed like a perfect swap.

I woke up the next morning thinking what have I done? *Oy chihuahua!*

I looked down quickly and breathed a sigh of relief. I must have remembered in time that I'm scared of needles and that I have three children whom I've banned from even having a ladybird tattooed on their ankles until they're 18 and officially beyond my control.

I backed out of the swap, but now I paint the bust as a tattooed self-portrait.

I went back for the party and charity auction and I got a bit carried away by the atmosphere of the event. I forgot that I wanted to surf monster waves and have attitude. Instead I behaved like a surf chick playing imaginary volleyball.

And if I was a surf chick, the next logical move was to find a dude.

Destiny was smiling on me. I turned to the bar to grab another drink and there in front of me was the perfect victim. Mr Right was probably right behind him, but my view was blocked by a pyramid of Tahitian beer cans.

I don't know what happened, but the recoupling rulebook went out of the window. The perfect victim didn't have the qualities I was meant to be looking for: sensible job, similar age, compatible children, but he did have messy blond hair, pale blue eyes, sexy LA accent. I forgot about the restructured family and my responsibility to my friends to find another suitable dinner party guest; all I could think about was waxing each other's boards, rubbing suncream onto each other's backs and drinking weak beer in the Californian sunset.

'Hi, what are you doing here?' he asked.

'I just brought my bust in. Would you like to see it?' Smooth. Then he tells me, 'I'm the auctioneer.'

I notice that the bust of my breasts has been decorated with targets, and I wonder if it would be a good conversational gambit to tell him the surreal but hugely entertaining story about the theft of my bust. I could make out that those unnaturally perfect world champion's ones hanging on the wall are mine. Or would that be a little sad?

It's hard to get back into the dating thing after 15 years, but I must be able to come up with a better line than, 'Would you like to see my bust?'

Never mind, it works; we exchange phone numbers and I go home to make dinner for the kids pretending I have another party lined up.

AM I A CHICK?

It soon occurs to me that the only difference between mature dating and immature dating is that instead of trying to make sure your parents don't find out, you try to make sure your kids don't find out.

I'm not sure that this flirtation is a good idea, so I go round for a cup of tea one morning with the intention of telling Surf Dude that I'm not ready for any kind of relationship, but he looks like he'd make a lousy cup of tea, so I go to bed with him instead.

I find that bit easy enough (even though, according to women's magazines, it's meant to be the hard part), so the rest of the repartnering ritual should be a walk in the park. Regardless of anyone's theories, I've worked out my own three-point plan for choosing a man. It's simple enough; these are the essential qualities I'm looking for in a potential new boyfriend:

1. Laid-back attitude.

2. About half a million euros (at least) in the bank. I'm a surf bum *and* an artist so I need expensive cadmium pigments, 24-carat gold leaf, longboards, designer wetsuits and boat trips in the Mentawai islands.

3. Cold beer in the fridge.

The last point seemed important because I wrote the list on the beach on a very hot day and I was kind of thirsty. But, after all, what use would I have for a man who didn't keep a cold beer handy?

I'm not sure about point two either: money's not crucial, I was only trying to be sensible. Point one is crucial, and Surf Dude is the most laid-back person I've ever met and he owns a bar, which makes him OK for beer. So what could go wrong?

Personally I only have one of the three things on my list (unless I drank it last night). I start stressing out. Maybe I'm not doing enough yoga? Maybe I'm doing too much yoga and I've succeeded in erasing my ego altogether? You would think the Surf Dude situation was perfect: nice-looking man in flip-flops, no socks, no intention of ever going to a dinner party with me, no children.

I ring my sister. 'It's pointless, it will never work, he's much younger than me and he's gorgeous.'

'What is your problem? You prefer ugly old men?'

'No, it's just that he could be seeing a 20-year-old bikini model.'

'Why would he want to see a 20-year-old bikini model when he could be seeing you?' There's no hint of irony in her voice.

'Oh, I don't know. Maybe she'd look better in a bikini than me?' (When did I get it into my head that men *mind* if you can't fit into an extra-large bikini top? I must be feeling very negative.)

'So what? It's winter. Repeat after me, I am a goddess. I am a goddess.' Bless her, she's trying so hard. I've no doubt in my mind that my sister is a goddess, but I'm not so sure about myself.

And then there's the lifestyle thing. He tells me he doesn't count it as a late night if he's home before dawn; I sometimes find it hard to stay up until it's dark, let alone until it's light.

He comes back from a New Year extreme snowboard event where he's been working.

'So we're up on the glacier all day in a hundred and forty-kilometre-an-hour winds filming the snowboard contest, partied all night, back up for some snowboarding before work, back to the contest, partied all night, back up to the glacier and then what did we do that night, hang on… oh yes, partied all night then back up the glacier. What have you been up to?'

'I've been drinking a lot of carrot juice.' It's hard to explain this irrational behaviour. Did I get carried away with the training? Was I trying to fulfil the stereotype of the noble and long-suffering single mother, a role that my children can't stand?

'Mum, you're not much fun are you?' is their reaction to my occasional dry spells. 'Can't you go over to Taryn's house and ask her to mix you a White Russian?' Or maybe it was the influence of my antecedents who were Methodist missionaries. It's hard to kick the guilt habit, although I try, I really do. But carrot juice is taking it too far, it's dangerous: you can get vitamin A poisoning and go orange.

'I've been doing quadrilateral equations.' I really did spend New Year's Eve helping Daisy revise for a maths exam – she got ten per cent.

'And we got a new rat.' Wow! I'm beginning to think I need therapy. This man certainly needs therapy if he wants to go on seeing me.

I keep cancelling dates because I need to do something like clean out the hamster cages. This sounds crazy now even to me, but the hamsters were important to the emotional well-being of my children after we came down from Walton's Mountain.

One night Surf Dude rings from a crowded bar. I can hear a lot of glamorous bikini models partying in the background. He asks if I'm coming for a beer.

'Sorry, I've got to stay home and watch *Cinderella*.'

'*Cinderella* again?'

What can I say? It's Alice's favourite and she wants me to watch it with her. I thought the beer could wait, but he's right, I should know the plot by now. Girl meets boy, she loses her shoe, but she keeps her man. What Cinderella does *not* do is mess up by staying home watching Disney cartoons and cleaning out hamster cages.

RETAIL THERAPY

I know I shouldn't take it too badly when he ends it, it wasn't meant to be *l'amour fou*, but I don't do casual very well and it has been about 20 years since I was dumped. Anyway, what's the point of getting dumped if you can't indulge in some artistic depression, moan to your friends and swap organic carrot juice for rum punch?

I could go to my masseuse for a hypnotherapy session and conjure up some laughing dolphins, instead I choose retail therapy, not for the kids this time, for myself. If I were in *Sex and the City* I would buy a new pair of Jimmy Choo's. This is Biarritz and it's February. I've decided only a new wetsuit will secure my emotional well-being.

It's more than just retail therapy, its thalassotherapy – a seawater massage cure popular in Biarritz in luxury spas, or you can opt for the cheaper do-it-yourself version – jumping in the ocean. I've been waiting impatiently for the Mamas to start up again in the spring, but I can't wait. It's time to cut the umbilical cord, which is made of some super-strength plastic with a Velcro fastening.

I set off up the *route nationale* towards Bayonne. The first shop I get to is called Under Eighteen Only. I look in the rear-view mirror. No, I'm not going to get away with it. I drive past and on to the Chambre d'Amour in Anglet, the Chamber of Love. Sounds promising.

I go into a hip-looking place and walk past the counter where a group of super-cool young guys are watching a kamikaze skateboard video and listening to my favourite thrash metal track. The till is covered with stickers saying things like 'Ride It Scum', 'Youth Against Establishment' and 'Skate Or Die'.

I try to erase the Dolly Parton song I've been listening to in the car from my mind and get into my hard core head.

I walk over to the women and children's rail. I'm trying to work out which is which when a guy with long black ringlets and green eyes comes over; his T-shirt says 'If You Can't Rock And Roll, Fuck Off'. If he were my son I'd tell him to pull his trousers up because I can see his boxers, but he's not, so I admire the rather original skull and hibiscus pattern on them instead.

'Can I help you with anything at all?'

Yes, you can give me a massage, I'm feeling stressed out.

I state the obvious. 'I'm looking for a wetsuit.'

'You're in the right place. Who's it for? Your son *peut-être*?'

Damn, do I look old enough to have children? 'No, it's for me as a matter of fact.'

'Oh, OK. Are you going somewhere or is it for summer *peut-être*?'

'No, it's for here, right now, this afternoon.'

157

'Oh, OK. You're a good surfer then? There's a big swell running.'

I can't start lying so early in our relationship.

'No, I'm crap.'

'Why don't you wait until the summer then? It's much better for learning.'

I'm getting sick of this. Does he really need to know I've been spending too much time with my family and my hamsters? Stop asking questions, give me the wetsuit or give me your phone number.

'It's all right, I'll wait until the swell drops, I promise. Will this fit me?'

'Probably not, that's for *age* twelve.'

He takes me to the women's section, finds me a suit, zips me up and tells me it looks great. The flattery might be his selling patter, but I'm sufficiently charmed to part with more money than I've ever spent on an outfit in my life.

I keep my word and wait until it's flat, then I ring around my friends to drag someone out there with me. I get a lot of fake-sounding excuses.

'I'm having lunch in Spain.'

'I've just put a chicken in the oven.'

'I'm doing the ironing.'

'I've got to stay home and watch *Cinderella*.'

I'm feeling insecure; not even my friends want to come out and play.

I call Taryn, and at last I get to the truth.

'Wilma, it's fucking freezing. It's February. You can come round and get in the Jacuzzi if you want.'

'No, I think I'll go and have a surf anyway.' Why? Why? Why? I could choose the Jacuzzi, one of Taryn's famous cranberry and vodka sundowners and enjoy a chat about life, love and board wax. Or I could face frostbite alone.

I feel shaky as I turn down Taryn's attractive offer. The truth is I've never been surfing by myself before. I've walked into the water when everyone's on the beach and stuff, but I've never tied the board on the roof rack alone and set off to surf the unridden wave in the middle of winter.

I tell the kids, 'I'm just going for a surf.'

'It's freezing, Mum. Who are you going with?'

'Oh, nobody.'

They look at each other. 'Are you sure you'll be all right? We'll come and watch if you like, but it's a bit cold.'

'Hahaha. It's OK, I am a *grown up*.' I try and make that sound convincing. My actual mental age is probably about 17: I liked a boy and he didn't like me, so I bought a wetsuit and I'm going for a surf. So there.

As I walk down from the car park, I'm waiting for someone to tap me on the shoulder and say, 'You can't do this, you should be home baking scones.'

I should explain that I'm not completely crazy – even I would class the waves out there as small, it's the idea that it's my first solo flight that's making it seem like such a monumental and heroic event. When I surf with Christophe, even on the days when the swell gets over 60 centimetres, I feel safe. I have confidence in him and know deep down that he's not going to let me die. He may get pissed off with me from time to time – when I run over him in the water or when my dog pees on his cooler – but I'm pretty sure he's not trying to get rid of me. Paddling out alone is a whole new challenge.

Despite the swell being so tiny the sea seems full of danger. I imagine what is lurking under the smooth glassy surface of the water: weaver fish, octopus, great white sharks, giant squid. And somewhere down there with the bottom feeders – the hagfish and the eyeless sea slugs – is my insecurity, my fear of failure. The feeling that I'm not good enough; not good enough for the Gagosian Gallery or the Tate, for rollerblading or baking saffron buns. I'm just an idiotic middle-aged woman trying to recapture a lost youth she never had as a surf chick.

A bit further down the beach there are a couple of guys messing about in the glassy little waves. They get out, leaving me all alone. The beach is deserted, the sun is setting over the mountains in Spain, a few seagulls are flapping around; if I were a surf artist I could do an atmospheric if slightly corny painting of this moment. I do a few yogic breathing exercises to calm my nerves and then I set off and take a few good waves.

When I say 'good waves' I can see with hindsight that these weren't technically good waves, but at this point merely standing up was my goal, so these few good waves meant a great deal to me. They made me feel like the best surfer in the world – if the best surfer in the world *is* the one having the most fun.

After four waves in a row, I get a serious case of ice-cream head, so I get out before frostbite sets in. I drive home in my wetsuit and jump straight into a hot bath with a glass of rum.

My English surf buddy Jo calls while I'm thawing out in the coconut bubbles.

'Are you feeling OK?'

'OK? I'm feeling fucking wonderful. Four awesome waves and all by myself, how cool is that?'

'I meant about the dude?' Jo's been playing agony aunt all week.

'Oh, him. It wasn't exactly *l'amour fou*, was it? Don't you want to hear about my waves?'

The thalassotherapy seems to have worked a treat.

LET THEM EAT CAKE

The children definitely feel that France is their home now after three years. The turning point is when they say *'Oh là là'* spontaneously when they're surprised

Their French is fluent and annoyingly they have perfect accents, so my strong English accent is a constant source of amusement to them. My defence is to invoke the name of the mighty Jane Birkin (probably the most popular English person this side of the channel since Winston Churchill), which gives my accent instant sex appeal and stops everyone seeing me as a *rosbif* struggling with schoolbook French. It cuts no ice with my children; in the end I have to remind them that I taught them to talk in the first place to get any respect at all.

Daisy even sings in French. At 16 she starts a band; at 17 goes solo. I am filled with maternal pride when she reduces a woman at the Madrid Hotel to tears with her rendition of 'La Vie en Rose'. I am so overflowing with maternal pride I drink a lot of rosé to calm my nerves and become so overenthusiastic that Daisy tells me I'm an embarrassing stage mum and bans me from all future gigs.

When I ask the kids if I can help with their homework, they look at me as if I'm crazy.

'Sorry, Mum, I don't want to get zero per cent,' Nat says uncharitably, but he does ask me to test him on dates for history one evening. I'm not concentrating very hard (a hangover from my own history lessons) so I'm a bit confused when the topic 'Defeat at Waterloo' crops up.

'I think we won that one, darling,' I say.

'Who is *we*, Mum?' he laughs.

Me and the Duke of Wellington. Sorry, but I can't side with Napoleon even if our address is the Chemin de l'Empereur.

One thing we definitely approve of is that the French love a holiday. There are sometimes four bank holidays in May alone, and if the French don't feel that they've had enough days off, they call a general strike.

Bastille Day, 14 July, is the biggest holiday of the year. The sound of fireworks exploding and champagne corks popping will fill the air at midnight.

I don't know that much about the French Revolution, but I got the basics before I was chucked off history O-level. The story goes like this: Marie Antoinette is skipping around the Petit Trianon at Versailles dressed as a shepherdess, unaware of the starving mob at the palace gates. A courtier tells her, 'But, Your Highness, the peasants have no bread.' She supposedly utters the immortal line, 'Let them eat cake!' and the revolution is unleashed. This is probably urban legend and even if you want to believe it, it wasn't cake but brioche – a sweet eggy bread the French eat with jam for breakfast or with foie gras at the cocktail hour. (The queen hadn't picked up on the fact that the peasants were also out of foie gras and champagne.) The Bastille is stormed and 14 prisoners are released including the Marquis de Sade. The ideas of the Enlightenment descend in to the bloodbath of the Reign of Terror with the crone-like *tricoteuses* knitting in the shadow of Madame Guillotine, dropping a stitch every time a Royalist head falls.

I recently found out why these women were knitting. Secret trials were illegal under the constitution of the new republic, so these women were paid to show up and witness the proceedings. They brought their knitting to avoid boredom, like film extras. As the Reign of Terror went on, the macabre knitting circle realised that they weren't just witnesses to the trials, they had the power to influence the court's decision. So they sat there like the Fates with the power of life and death in their hands, and probably forgot the knitting for a bit.

But what were they knitting? String vests for the revolutionary army? Thermal underwear for the *sans-culottes*? Baby booties for the orphans of the guillotine?

Another question I can't help asking is whether we should be worried about the fact that ten years after the beginning of the revolution, Napoleon became dictator and five years after that he was made emperor?

I'm in favour of the end of the absolute power of the monarchy and the abolition of serfdom, and I'm really glad to be living in this classless society of liberty, equality and brotherhood.

So it was very disillusioning when Daisy told me about 'Nappy Rallies', an intriguing name that makes you wonder what the hell they might involve.

You could imagine something quite cool and revolutionary, a bunch of enlightened toddlers wandering up the Champs-Élysées carrying banners saying, 'Babies are born free, yet everywhere they are found in diapers.'

The truth is a very different, far darker thing, as I found out.

'How could you send me to a school where things like this go on?' asked Daisy.

'I don't know, I didn't have much choice, did I?' She started off in the local state school, but when she was 15 the school politely suggested that she ended her academic education and took up a practical training course. I politely suggested that I envisaged Daisy doing languages at one of the best universities in the world.

The headmaster played the *liberté, égalité, fraternité* card. 'In France, madame, unlike in your country, we have a classless society. We do not make distinctions between people. In our opinion there would be nothing wrong with Daisy doing a bricklaying course, it would be no better or worse than her attending the Sorbonne.'

I agree with the principle, but I have two problems with his idea. First, I wouldn't like to sign Daisy up to a profession where she might break a nail. Second, I would hate to be held responsible for anyone sitting under a wall she had built.

I politely suggest that they stuff it, and I enrolled her in the private Catholic school in St-Jean-de-Luz. It's against my principles, but the fees are only €150 a term and I enjoy writing the cheque out to St Thomas Aquinas, as if I might be buying a few favours in the afterlife, and the kids don't have to pretend to be Catholic.

'What's a Hindu?' Nat asked after his first catechism class.

I try to sound knowledgeable; I mutter something about reincarnation, elephant gods and tantric sex. Then I think that's unusually open-minded, teaching comparative religion on the first day. 'Why do you ask?'

'I told them we were Hindu, so they didn't think we were Catholic.'

'Why Hindu, if it's not a stupid question?'

'I thought it sounded cool. No one else in my class is Hindu.'

This religious tolerance isn't matched by tolerance for Daisy's slightly outrageous way of dressing, and I'm called into the school to sign a contract saying that I'll check her outfit as she leaves the house. They are obviously unaware that my shady past as a Neo Naturist makes my signature worthless. One morning the secretary takes Daisy into her office and removes her make up by force causing Daisy to be late for her first lesson.

Her note explaining 'reason for lateness' throws the physics teacher into complete confusion: 'Make-up removal by Mme Laroche.'

Overall I'm pretty happy with the school, but it seems I didn't check the place thoroughly enough and Daisy is fuming.

'I just can't believe you'd do this to me.'

What is going on in the corridors of St Thomas? Bullying, glue sniffing, drug dealing?

No, it's the *Jeunesse Dorée*, the Gilded Youth, an elitist freemasonry of high society teenagers, twenty-first-century debutantes. The idea is that they shouldn't mingle with people from lower social classes or income brackets, so their parents organise *rallyes* or private soirées for them to meet and mate in a protected environment, not mixing their blood with the commoners.

I was confused by this bourgeois *ancien régime* concept until I read the succinct explanation on one of their websites. '*Il ne fallait pas absolument se mélanger aux autres sous peine de contamination sociale*.' We should absolutely not mix with other people, to avoid risk of social contamination.

In Paris they are known as the NAPPYs, which comes from the initials of Paris's most chic districts: Neuilly, Autiel, Pereire and Passy. The NAPPYs seem blissfully unaware that the acronym exposes them to accusations of being full of shit.

On their blog they have two campaigns. Save the whales? Save the earth? No, of course not. One is 'Stop Le Fake – Say No to Fake Louis Vuitton'; the other is 'Stop the Tax on Private Jets'.

'God, I'm sorry. I had no idea, I hope you're not going to any of these rallies.'

Daisy laughs. 'Mum, I wouldn't go near them. They're inbred, moronic fascists and they're ugly. Apart from that, I don't think we exactly count as the *grande bourgeoisie* around here!'

What? Now I see red. These people are clearly the scum of the earth, but how dare they suggest Daisy isn't good enough for them?

'Why weren't these people guillotined in the Terror?'

I'm ready to get out my knitting. *Vive la Révolution!*

LET THEM BAKE CAKE

The spirit of *liberté, égalité, fraternité* still runs through the Mamas Surf Club. Surfing is not a financially elitist sport as all you need is a board and a block of wax, but there is elitism based on ability to ride the wildest waves and carry off the demigod – or goddess – look in the ocean. Money can't buy you respect in the line-up.

You do see a few jet-set surf millionaires round here and both Gucci and Chanel put out designer boards a few years ago, although I can't imagine anyone walking down the beach with one. A real 'designer board' is one made by a famous shaper, so a surfer wouldn't want a Chanel surfboard any more than a fashionista would want a little black dress designed by my shaper friend Phil Grace.

It can get pretty competitive out there, especially when you get a lot of men in the water with something to prove. The great thing about the Mamas Surf Club is that we're all women and we're all starting late; some are better than others but no one's ever won a big-wave trophy. We can come in on the same wave holding hands, displaying our solidarity. Cynicism hasn't set in; maybe a time will come when we become more hard-bitten: 'Get off my wave before you ding my board or break my nail, bitch!' But for the moment we're happy to congratulate each other and ourselves on awesome waves and superhuman stamina. It's great learning to surf with kindred spirits who understand concepts like fear, waterproof mascara and cake recipes.

Wait a minute – cake recipes?

'I thought it would be cool if everyone took it in turns to bake a cake for when we get out of the water,' suggested one of the Mamas.

Oh no, just when I've got to my feet. There's one thing I do worse than surfing – baking.

The children could tell them that; they never let me forget the last time I made a cake. It was a while back: a wet weekend in Baile na nGall. I had decided to have one last try for the title of Housewife of the Year.

I put on my apron and soon the smell of home baking wafts through the house. Daisy comes rushing into the kitchen.

'What on earth is that supposed to be?'

I get defensive. 'Daisy, you may know fifty Irish words for rain, but you have to improve your command of the English language. It is not "supposed to be" anything, it *is* a cake.'

'Are you sure? It doesn't look like one.'

'Mmmm.' She's got a point. 'Just read me the recipe again, I'll make sure I didn't forget anything.'

'Very Simple Idiot-Proof Sponge,' she says and lists the ingredients.

'OK. I did forget something.'

'What – the pinch of salt, the optional cinnamon?'

'The flour.'

There's only so much humiliation I can take on a Saturday afternoon. Anyway, I thought we were meant to be getting out of the kitchen and riding the wild surf.

'I'm not sure about this cake idea. Aren't we meant to be hard core, gnarly surf dudes?' I complain.

'That's the point, we're different. We don't have to be macho just because we surf.'

I don't know, I was thinking of having a Maori tattoo on my biceps. If I only had biceps.

'But I've got three children. It's hard.'

'Jo's got four and she can make raspberry pavlova.'

And stand up, I know. I hate to beg, but…

'Please, please can I buy a cake instead? Please?'

Maybe I should get a cake recipe tattooed on my arm. That way I wouldn't forget the flour.

In the end we agree that as long as the cake comes from the *boulangerie* and not the supermarket, bought cake is acceptable. I don't seem to have time for anything much apart from painting, surfing and my kids at the moment, and what's the point competing with pastry chefs in a country where they are as respected as philosophers, and a bloody revolution was unleashed after an insensitive remark about brioche?

Tea and cake is a pretty good thing to see when you come out of the water in cold weather, and they endear us even more to Christophe and the other instructors who are already glad that we're women, not screaming children who pee in their wetsuits. In warmer weather a packet of pistachio nuts and a cooler of rosé are a good substitute and require less effort.

I do arrive with a home-made cake on one occasion and it's a big success. At first I bask in the admiration of the other Mamas and the surf instructors, but I feel guilty and admit that my youngest daughter Alice made it.

OH *MERDE*...
REAL WAVES!

One sunny afternoon at the Mamas Surf Club everything seems to come together.

We're down at the naturist beach, but I've compromised for the sake of my fellow Mamas and surf instructors. The naturists look at my swimsuit with disapproval; I'm seen as a traitor.

'I'm learning to surf,' I explain to the naturists. This excuse gets me nowhere. If I must learn to surf, they seem to be thinking, I could at least do it naked. It would be so much more amusing.

I go out to join the women in the water, and take off on a huge wave. Well, it seems huge to me; remember waves do look a lot bigger from below, and everything is overhead when you're lying down. There's this massive wave behind me, I feel its momentum pick up the board and I stand up and ride it all the way in with foam flying all around me. I'm surrounded by Surf Mamas whistling and cheering.

'*Magnifique!*'

'*Belle vague!*' Beautiful wave!

'Awesome, dude!'

It's like the end of a feel-good Hollywood movie. Depressed housewife conquers fear, Guinness and childcare issues to surf monster wave, fade, cut, titles. There should be heroic music blasting out, 'The Ride of the Valkyries' or 'Surfin' Safari'. A group of bronzed naturists would form the chorus line, and the Mamas could take the solos. I should probably remain silent because I'm tone deaf.

I trip over my leash and do a bit of a bellyflop at the end, but it's still a champagne moment of my life in surf. I'm just about to head up the beach to see what the Mamas' cooler has to offer when Christophe breaks the spell.

'Not bad, Wilma. I think you're ready for a Real Wave.'

'Real wave? What on earth do you mean?' That was real enough for me; I still have some of it swirling round my sinuses as proof. France is the land of philosophy, and if Christophe's planning a debate about the nature of reality he's picked the wrong moment. I took an awesome wave and I want beer and flattery.

'I believe that was a Real Wave, Christophe,' I say with an airy laugh. 'It felt pretty wet.'

'But, Wilma, you're still in the mousse.'

The soundtrack screeches to a halt. I feel sick and sweaty suddenly. I know what he means. When you start surfing you stay in the whitewater near the shore, after the wave has broken and it is just finding its way slowly in to the beach. After that you go 'out back' to the deep water and catch the waves

173

before they break. These are Real Waves, or green waves; the whitewater is mousse. Like chocolate mousse or hair mousse, it's soft and unthreatening.

It doesn't always feel soft and unthreatening to me, but I can't really argue with Christophe while I'm standing in knee-deep water. But when did I say I wanted to surf Real Waves?

Doesn't he understand? I'm not a teenage boy modelling myself on a photo of a surf pro at a gnarly break called Killer's, Devil's Rock or Dracula's. I'm taking my inspiration from a vintage beer mat I bought in New York depicting a 1950s hula queen surfing a knee-high breaker into Waikiki Beach, holding a tray of cocktails over her head. That's the look I was aiming for and I feel as if I just got close – minus the grass skirt and pina coladas. Why spoil the moment? After all, I've got nothing to prove.

'Oh, Christophe, don't let's ask for the stars, we have the moon. It looks a bit big today, maybe next week.' Maybe next year, I think to myself.

'Wilma, you can't be scared, there are *children* out there… '

So what? We all know that children, cute and lovable as they are, are complete idiots where danger is concerned. That's why parents spend half their lives trying to stop their offspring running into roads, shutting themselves into fridges or re-enacting the stunts from *Jackass* in the living room.

Sure, I can see them. I can hear them too, laughing and shouting *'Oh là là!'* when a big set rolls through. I rest my case. Idiots.

'… and other Mamas,' I hear him say. The surf club is completely non-competitive, that's the beauty of it being a women-only, testosterone-free zone. It's all about encouraging each other and boosting each other's egos, sharing our waves and make-up tips. We don't care if our friends are better at surfing any more than we care if they're richer, thinner and more successful. Do we?

Hmmm, maybe I have got something to prove after all.

'OK, I'll come out and have a look.'

Getting out there is half the fun. Down here they call it 'passing the bar', which adds an extra level of stress as if you might have to take legal exams while you paddle.

I finally get out and comfort myself with the thought that as I am grown up, no one can force me to do anything I don't want to do. Christophe may be able to *suggest* I take a scary, green, unbroken wave, but he can't make me do it. I'm in control of my destiny, or so I thought.

I start to feel a bit seasick and regret having left the security of the beach and the cooler of beer so far behind. The waves seem mountainous and menacing, blocking out the sunlight. It's as if they've travelled thousands of kilometres across the ocean from the coast of Brazil specifically to pick me up like flotsam or jetsam and toss me onto the sand at the feet of a passing nudist.

'You know what, I'm a bit tired and thirsty, I think I'll just go in now.'

'I don't think so.' He grabs me by the leash and pulls me after him like a wet poodle. 'Come on, it's only sixty centimetres.'

That's a matter of opinion.

You never paddle back in to the beach. The point being that you should try and fail rather than not try at all. It's better to wipeout, it shows commitment and you'll get in quicker.

Quicker? Maybe. In one piece? Maybe not. I can see I'm not going to escape until I give it a go.

Here's the theory: I take off on the wave just as it breaks. When I feel the board pick up speed, I do a little press-up and jump to my feet. Then I turn either left or right, away from the whitewater, and surf across the face of the wave. I turn up and down the wave, carving a zigzag line of white foam behind me like the mark of Zorro.

Here's the reality: Christophe pushes me into a wave (this makes life a lot easier if you have no biceps). I clamber to my feet and stay standing for a couple of seconds, then I part company with my board and I am catapulted into the water and swirled around like an insect that's accidentally flown into a Jacuzzi. I try to remember all the advice I've been given. Don't try to breathe underwater. Keep your hands over your face so you don't break your nose. Don't hold the leash or it will snap off your fingers. Don't get the leash caught round your neck or it will strangle you. Don't pee in case there are great white sharks nearby (that applies more to Australia, I guess, but the sharks might have got lost on their migration route). And above all, don't panic.

I surface waterlogged and spluttering after what is probably 20 seconds but feels like 30 minutes. I make a general apology to anyone near enough to hear me. I hit my head on something underwater and I'm not sure whether it was my board, someone else's board or someone else's head. Or was it the glass ceiling that separates a real surfer from someone who once stood up in the mousse?

Reality might not sound as glamorous as the theory, but during my two and a half seconds standing on the face of the wave, I have seen the possibility of being a Real Surfer who surfs Real Waves. I'm like someone who's been through a near-death experience and become a born-again Christian. I've been through a near-surf experience and I've seen the light.

Not everyone takes to it. It's like getting drunk. Some people wake up the following morning thinking: I feel sick, I've got a headache, I made a complete fool of myself, I'll never do that again. Some of us wake up wondering: How long until six o'clock?

I feel sick, I've got a headache and I made a complete fool of myself. I want another wave.

I paddle back out to Christophe.

'Again, again.' In the end he has to drag me back in, reminding me that there's cold beer on shore and the sun is setting.

He's created a monster.

SUIVEZ LES MAMAS!

The Mamas Surf Club gets quite well known, other women join and other clubs set up in St-Jean-de-Luz and the neighbouring villages. We're pleased because one of our aims – apart from turning ourselves into extreme sport Bond Girls – was to get more women in the water. But we do make it clear that we are the original Mamas Surf Club, and one weekend a journalist comes down from Paris to write an inspirational piece about us for a women's magazine.

One of the exciting things about surfing is the unpredictable nature of it: you never surf the same wave twice. You can go back to the same beach with the same size swell running at the same stage of the tide and not recognise the place. The wind direction may have changed, the swell coming from a different place at a different speed, the waves a different shape, the sea a different colour. A butterfly flaps its wings on the other side of the world and everything you thought you knew about surfing has to be thrown out of the window.

Its unpredictability is part of the fun, but at this exact moment with the journalist and the photographer on the beach it doesn't seem like fun at all.

On the way to the beach I felt quite confident of dazzling everyone with my new ability to surf Real Waves. The conditions have changed and I'm literally wrong-footed. Here I am trying to inspire oppressed French housewives to get 'Out of the kitchen and into the surf' and I seem to have totally lost my superpowers – I can no longer walk on water. Just when I thought I was getting somewhere I'm back to where I started, before mastering the press-up, bellyflopping around in the white wash swearing a lot.

The waves are not huge and scary, they're just weird; they seem to be coming from a strange angle and breaking wherever they feel like it, which is usually on my head. Every time I take a wave it changes direction and chucks me off like a bucking bronco. As I get more and more tired and frustrated I become more desperate to prove myself, but with every fall the possibility of redemption and a good action shot diminishes.

Nobody is on top of their game, but Christophe has saved the day by offering to take the blonde journalist tandem surfing, and I don't think she cares what the Mamas are doing any more.

'How's it going Wilma?' he asks coming in and seeing me crumpled on the sand like the broken woman that I am.

'*Catastrophique,*' I say snivelling in a waterlogged and defeated way.

'Ah, come on, I'll take you out.'

If someone offers to take you tandem surfing it will involve paddling out with his head practically on your bum, it's the only way you will both fit on the board. Don't let this put you off, but don't wear a G-string and don't go out with some random perv who wants to get a better look at the stitching on your bikini bottoms. Christophe once ranked second in the world tandem championships in Hawaii and I'm wearing a wetsuit, so I jump at the offer.

I was inspired to surf partly by that postcard of Christophe, in the classic pose, holding his daughter above his head, so it's the fulfilment of an ambition. Although I'm a bit disappointed when he tells me I'm a little heavy for that move. Never mind, we paddle out on the long two-man board and he effortlessly catches the wave, jumps up and lifts me to my feet. The next thing I know I am standing on the board, turning up and down the wave, carving turns, doing cut-backs and cruising down the line. It's like magic, an illusion – Christophe is doing everything, but it's like suddenly being really good at surfing. I am turning like a former French champion. I may never turn that well again. It's an insight into how things should be.

Later in the bar my tandem partner and I have a difference of opinion. The journalist asks us what is the single most important aspect of learning to surf. Christophe and I answer at the same time. I say something about empowerment, feeling good about yourself and discovering the goddess within.

Christophe says, 'Abs.'

There's an argument to be made that his method is more successful than mine, but I like the following quote from a big wave guru about surfing: 'It's ninety-nine per cent in your head, but the other one per cent has to be completely fit.' He may have been talking about 10-metre Hawaiian breakers, but it holds for the 60-centimetre ankle busters as well.

Christophe and I agree (as I eventually accepted in my yoga class) you need abs and the inner goddess.

A couple of months later I'm in the supermarket and I see the headline on the cover of a magazine: *'Peur des vagues? Suivez les Mamas Surfeuses!'* Scared of waves? Follow the Surf Mamas!

If they'd seen me last week losing it in the line up at Centiz the magazine may have changed the headline to: 'Scared of waves? Follow the Surf Mamas right out of the water and into the bar.' The story on the Mamas is in a section called 'psy & co', not to be read 'psycho' whatever my children might think. Crazy Surf Mamas!

I look inside, there we are bonding with each other, overcoming our fear of waves and our fear of having photos of ourselves wearing bikinis on every French supermarket till from Calais to Cannes. We are sending a message to women all over the country to abandon their trolleys, tell their husbands to go to McDonald's and head out into the water.

'Oh look – that's me,' I say to Daisy as casually as I can.

'Great! Oh, are you decent this time?'

Daisy recently came back from the village bar and asked me in mock horror, 'Have you any idea what it's like going out for a meal and seeing a semi-pornographic photo of your mother hanging on the wall?'

Can't say I have, but I can explain. The photo was a present for Patrique, who had thrown a party for the Mamas in his bar.

'Fine, but why are all the other women wearing wetsuits and holding boards while you're lying on the ground in a pin-up pose in a bikini?'

'I had a bad back, I could hardly stand up even on the beach.' This is absolutely true and I'd have much rather been surfing than sunbathing, but it did make a funny picture. I check the pictures in the magazine. Yes, all decent. I slip a copy in the trolley sensing I've finally done something to impress my teenage daughter.

'We'll take two,' she says loudly, 'because my mother – this is her – is in the magazine. She's a SURFER.'

I check out the trolley of the woman behind. Foie gras, *le rosbif*, champagne, a copy of *Vie Pratique Madame*.

Ah, once she's read the story she'll fling the shopping on the kitchen floor and say to her husband: 'You cook for your parents. I'm going out to buy a longboard!'

I read the complete article when I get home.

Johanna explains how she'd come from the ski world where everyone is on the slopes and was shocked to see how few women there were in the water. She decided it was time to overthrow the macho system.

'What does surf mean to us?' the magazine asks.

We all talk about how we overcame our fear and how it has changed our lives, but my favourite quote is from Florence who answered simply, 'Freedom!'

BLACK MOON

I'm not even thinking about finding a soul mate when I meet the next man. In fact I'm not thinking about anything at all because it's three o'clock in the morning and I'm fast asleep. I've been out to dinner, drunk too much wine and gone to bed when Bibi starts barking and howling. I get downstairs to find her throwing herself against the back door in a frenzy.

For once Bibi is not just giving in to her Gothic paranoia. I let her out thinking it's most likely a cat but this time there *really are* people in my garden. I'm now in a confusing situation: I have let the dog out to scare off intruders. Am I meant to follow her out? I hate the idea of sacrificing my faithful hound to some mad axe man wandering round the hydrangeas, but I sure as hell don't want to sacrifice myself with her.

Bibi won't come in, so I shut the door, grab the phone to ring the police and open the window to see what's going on. The intruders seem to be going into the studio at the end of the garden where my friend Igor works.

'Igor?'

183

'Ah, yes, Wilma. Good evening, would you like a glass of wine?'

'Oh, sure.' It's probably either a bit late or way too early for a drink, but it's such a relief to find it's Igor not a mad axe man. I put on an old bathrobe and go out.

What did I say about never, ever going out in Olatua without checking your look?

All the bars have closed and Igor is raiding his cellar with a man who seems to neatly fill a surfer-shaped vacuum in my life. Blond, blue eyes, designer stubble, six-foot-something. Oh no, am I like one of those middle-aged men who always goes for the young blonde?

This guy appears to be a couple of years older than the Surf Dude. At this rate I'll be going out with someone my age five dudes down the line.

I like a bit of atmosphere and there's plenty tonight; the scene is like an old Hammer Horror movie: full moon, owls hooting, ivy growing over the turrets of the house. Bibi's doing an Oscar-winning performance as a werewolf. When she's wound up she's like a rabid pyjama case, but tonight she's raised her game. Igor is an aristocratic Parisian artist, so he's playing the count wearing a silk cravat and serving wine. In this garden shed drama, I'm *The Woman in White* – a white bathrobed Morticia.

The man turns out to be writing a book about a trip he took round the world on his motorbike. Did I dream this? A travel writer *and* a biker who surfs and looks like a Viking. He seems to be under the delusion that he's from a family of New Jersey cops with German roots, but I'm convinced that he can trace his ancestors back to Leif Eriksson. I call him Thorvald. We polish off a few more bottles and I go back to bed at dawn thinking the search is over, all I have to do now is sit back and wait.

So I wait. And wait. He's living in the village, so he can't really avoid me, but nothing happens. Well, not the earth shattering romance I was expecting.

He seems interested. We go out for drinks, meet at barbecues, go swimming and surfing and we even go to the local disco together. It's a long time since I went to a disco and an even longer time since I went to one with strobe lights that turn your teeth and underwear ultraviolet. The Unicorn is not a place I'd consider going to sober, and the doormen probably wouldn't let you in if you *were* sober anyway. We end up there after the local bars close, drink whisky all night and dance to Eurotrash hits of the 1980s. Thorvald's not very good at reading signals. I am standing in front of him, my underwear flashing and the disco ball is acting as a romantic reminder of the full moon under which we met, but still nothing changes between us.

Maybe I'm not good at reading the signs. I'm so convinced that he's the perfect man I invent all kinds of excuses for him, and months go by and still nothing happens. 'I've got an instinct,' I tell my friends who are worried about my blind optimism, then Thorvald goes to the Outer Hebrides. Can't I take a hint?

'It's all right, I don't think he likes hot weather.'

Eventually he comes back and finally makes a move. He asks me if I'd like to go to Urdax, a village in the mountains just across the Spanish border. (Actually I think he asked me if I knew anyone who'd like to go to Urdax and I proposed myself.) He's thinking of buying a piece of land there and he wants to check out the nightlife before committing. I could have saved him the petrol and told him that since there are only five houses in the place, the nightlife isn't likely to be as good as in, for instance, my back garden. I don't want to save him the petrol. I want to go to Urdax with Thorvald.

Here's one of the tragic things about being a surfer. Although this guy has lived in Manhattan, London and Amsterdam and travelled round the world on a motorbike, he's willing to give the nightlife in Urdax a chance because it's only 23½ minutes from the wave. We check that figure in the car on the way up.

The beer's fine, but there's no one in the bar at Urdax other than Thorvald, the barman – an old Basque man who looks as if he laughs once a year at Halloween – and me. I point out that this is as good as nightlife gets in Urdax because *I* wouldn't usually be here, and he would be alone with the barman, Lurch.

There are a couple of posters on the wall: one for the annual sheep show and one for the witches' convention in Zugguramundi. I always thought that the convention sounded exotic and intriguing until a friend told me that it's a bunch of Spanish goth girls in black leggings getting drunk on cider.

After a few beers we head back down to the coast, the bright lights of the village and the Bar Basque. I get drunk enough to feel it's time to stop all the bullshit and bare my soul. I come out with some classy line like, 'I fancy you,' or 'If you want to go back to Urdax for that sheep fair, I'm really into rare breeds.'

He tells me he's sorry, but he's going out with a Russian supermodel he met on his way to the Outer Hebrides or something. (I'm not sure that he said supermodel; he might have said woman.)

'Are you sure Russia's on the way to the Outer Hebrides?' I say sharply, but without losing my cool.

'No, no, I met her in a health food store in Amsterdam. Her bicycle broke down.'

Oh, no, now he's gone too far. That's just so, so, I don't know, virtuous. It's so organic and pesticide free and un-drunk.

I lose it completely. I tell him exactly what I think of men, Russian supermodels, health food shops and bicycles and then storm off into the night.

I wake up with a sick, empty feeling. Something's missing. Oh yes: my brain, my liver and any last vestiges of self-respect. This is a moral hangover.

I can't remember exactly what I screamed at him before my zigzag exit from his life, but I comfort myself with the thought that anyone who happened to be in the Bar Basque, the hotel or anywhere near the centre of the village could probably enlighten me. Oh, well, never mind, I'll probably never see him again. It's easy to avoid people in a village with one street.

I head shakily in to the village to buy a croissant and find that Thorvald's already in the Xpresso coffee bar eating a kebab special. This is a good sign; people usually resist the special until lunchtime unless they're very hungover. Perhaps he's had a total blackout and still remembers me as a relatively sane woman who likes rare breeds.

'Are you OK? You seemed a bit upset last night.'

Damn.

There's an awkward silence while I weigh up the idea of pretending I have a loopy identical twin.

Philippe, who runs the place, comes to my rescue. *'Ça va?'*

'Not really. Not at all.'

'Ah, the black moon. It drives people crazy like the mistral.'

And how, I think. 'Yeah, I'm sensitive to that kind of thing. Lunar energy, Saturn returns, pressure drops, beer.' I laugh a grim and mirthless laugh.

'But… ' Philippe is trying to cheer me up '… it can be good for *l'amour*!'

'Not in this case I'm afraid. Wrong kind of black moon.'

Thorvald laughs. 'Want a bite of my kebab? It's a great hangover cure.'

If you can't give me everlasting love or an Alka-Seltzer, I guess a bite of kebab will do for now.

The real story about the supermodel and the bike comes out later during a platonic beer-drinking marathon. He met and became friends with my ex-husband before he met me, and felt it would be complicated to ask me out. He went to the Outer Hebrides to think things through. That's when the Russian vegetarian got a flat tyre in Amsterdam and, like that butterfly flapping its wings somewhere, changed the course of my destiny. Oh well, *que sera sera* as Doris Day would say, at least I haven't become delusional.

He goes back to Amsterdam and I get back in the water thinking I really should forget the search for the perfect man and concentrate on the search for the Perfect Wave.

ENJOY THE WIPEOUT

'But rather, ten times rather, die in the surf, heralding the way to that new world, than stand idly on the shore.'

Florence Nightingale said that and Florence Nightingale can't be wrong. I was brought up in the cult of the Lady of the Lamp; the Ladybird book was my bedtime reading and we studied the heroic nurse year after year at school. I'm sure the school would have taken us on a trip to the Crimea if they could have arranged it, but at this moment standing in the rain on the promenade at Hendaye, I have to question the lady's judgement.

It's the beginning of November and the last session of the Mamas. The sea is an unattractive shade of khaki and the beach is covered with the kind of brown foam that you persuade yourself is 'algae' when you really want to get in. There's a swell running that looks huge.

I'm standing right outside the Serge Blanco Thalasso and Spa Institute wondering if I couldn't just nip in there instead? I could have a saltwater Jacuzzi and a seaweed scrub, a little session on the sunbed and have some blonde streaks. Wouldn't that be an easier way of achieving the surf-chick look?

The Mamas Surf Club has been reduced to Jo and me, the English contingent. I guess we're used to this sort of weather; whenever it gets like this people ask: 'But don't you love this weather, surely it reminds you of home?'

'Yes, it does,' I explain, 'that's why I left.'

Jo was also brought up with the cult of Florence Nightingale, freezing cold beaches and suffering for your pleasure. She's a nurse, which could come in handy if I go into shock or have a panic attack on the way out.

'We could always go to Spain for some tapas,' I suggest. We're right on the border, we could be there in five minutes, safely ensconced in some nice little bar with a plate of octopus salad and a bottle of Rioja.

But what would Ms Nightingale think about that? Not only idling on the shore but imbibing alcohol as well?

Not even Christophe and Johanna are here; they're away on their honeymoon, leaving us with another instructor, Xabi. He's a very nice man, but a little tough. It's not hard to get other instructors from the surf school to step in – we're considered a softer option than the delinquent teenagers who are sent down annually by the French government for a week's coaching.

'Where's everyone else?' Xabi asks, as if he can't think of anything anyone would rather do on a horrible Saturday afternoon in November.

Probably home in bed with a nice video and a cup of hot cocoa. Good plan.

Christophe and Johanna are on a yacht in New Zealand. Really good plan.

'Hey, Xabi, let's get married. We could go away on our honeymoon. Right now.'

'What?'

'OK, I'll get my wetsuit on,' I say grumpily. I don't handle rejection well. 'Well, maybe I'll just stay in the whitewater,' I add as we walk across the beach.

'Hahaha.' Xabi mistakenly thinks I'm joking. 'I haven't come out from St-Jean-de-Luz and put on a wet wetsuit so you can piss about in the mousse.'

'Waves are not measured in feet and inches, they are measured in increments of fear,' the big-wave surfer Buzzy Trent once said. He was talking about riding the biggest waves yet surfed on the north shore of Hawaii, but though my waves are smaller, my increments of fear are just as real as his.

I've no idea why I'm doing this. I feel so scared that I think I might actually throw up in the water. This isn't the same sort of day as my first trip 'out back' with Christophe earlier in the year. There's a 1.5-metre swell, and unless we really mess up we'll be surfing the face, which is up to twice that height.

Above me, on the sea wall separating the river from the sea and Spain from France, couples walk arm in arm, wearing hats and scarves and coats buttoned against the November rain, carrying umbrellas. They seem to be laughing, but that might just be paranoia. I feel like shouting up: Throw me a rope, your scarf, anything, get me out of here.

'There's nothing to worry about. Just stay close to the wall or you'll get caught by the waves. But not too close or you'll get smashed against the rocks,' Xabi warns us.

I look across the beach. The waves are breaking right across the bay, there's a current pulling us out by the breakwater, but the only way to get back in is through them, or I could stay out here until the swell dies down.

When I do get out there, I sit as far away from where the waves are breaking as possible. Xabi seems to think I'm in the wrong place, but it's a matter of opinion.

'Oh Wilma, what's the matter, don't you want to come over here and see me?' he laughs as if we were on the dance floor and I was acting coy.

The trouble with surfing is that there's only one way to get it right and so many ways to get it wrong. Only one right place to be, one right moment to take the wave, so many ways to fuck up.

Sit too far out and you'll never get a wave, too far in and it will break on top of you before you get a chance to take it; stand up too soon and you're left standing on the back of it with a 'nearly' feeling, too late and the nose of the board digs in and you're catapulted over the front of it into the trough.

I try most of these moves during the afternoon.

I may be listening to my coach's advice about weight distribution and positioning for take-off, but I'm getting my main inspiration from Samuel Beckett: 'Try again. Fail again. Fail better.'

By the end of the afternoon I'm failing pretty well, taking some spectacular wipeouts.

Surfers tell you that you have to learn to enjoy the wipeout. I've never seen what there is to enjoy about being swirled around underwater after a humiliating bellyflop, swallowing litres of saltwater and plankton. But it gets a lot better once I stop worrying about it and relax. The questions you might be asking are why would I want to spend my weekend doing this, and is there something slightly masochistic about it? After a few hours I realise that I have got over my fear of failure, I'm getting a little bit less scared with each wipeout.

By this time Xabi is probably ready for beer and tapas himself.

'Watch out, there's a big set coming. Are you scared? Is your heart beating a little faster?' he says challengingly.

Am I scared? No. I'm out here in big waves and I'm not scared any more, it's a lovely feeling. Perhaps that's a slight exaggeration or perhaps I should say I'm reasonably scared, adrenalin scared, but the point is I'm no longer completely terrified. I feel like someone who has faced her worst nightmares and woken up without wetting the bed.

I find myself laughing hysterically. I think I'm light-headed from swallowing seawater or an overdose of adrenalin and negative ions.

I take one more wave and one final wipeout and then I lie down and belly board in to the beach. I seem to be more or less in one piece, although I'm sure I'll find some interesting bruises when I take my wetsuit off, my ears are full of toxic water and my feet are a nasty pale green with cold.

By the time Jo reaches me I've got a *Little Miss Sunshine* smile glued to my face and I'm tap-dancing across the sand, humming a tune from the *Wizard of Oz*.

'You look happy. Deranged,' Jo says. 'What happened – did you get a good wave or hit your head on an octopus or something?'

'No, but I learned to enjoy the wipeout.'

By the time I get back to the Addams Family Mansion it's dusk and a thunderstorm has moved in. My children are there to greet me. Daisy is stretched out on the sofa; she could be the peroxide-blonde ghost of Marilyn Monroe except that she's reading the complete works of Racine in French. Nat is annihilating the forces of evil on a computer game and Alice is baking chocolate brownies.

Things seem to be the wrong way round in this house.

The kids like to surf in the summer, but they're not as obsessed as I am. The beach atmosphere can be pretty competitive with the surf world equivalent of ballet mums pushing their children out there. Not surfing is what kids do to rebel against their parents here.

I'm certainly not going to force the kids. It's wonderful being out in the ocean if you're in the mood, but if you're not it's a complete nightmare.

'Where on earth have you been?' Daisy asks when I come in. I sense disapproval as if I was the teenager and I'd come home at five in the morning with smudged lipstick and an empty tequila bottle.

It's pretty obvious where I've been. My wetsuit is leaving puddles on the kitchen floor and I have my board under my arm.

I say it anyway. 'Surfing.'

'Isn't it really big out there? Weren't you scared?' Their attitude to my surfing has changed from mild embarrassment to occasionally being quite proud of me.

'Not really.' A slight lie, but it takes a lot to impress teenagers so I can't miss the opportunity. 'Can someone pass me a beer and run me a bath?'

'Oh my God, what has happened to our MOTHER?' Daisy laughs.

'Do you remember when she was all squishy and she used to make tortillas?' Alice joins in.

I appreciate the past tense on the squishy bit; you still wouldn't bruise yourself on my abs.

'Oh yes, and she made us banana loaf at the weekends.' This is beginning to sound like *Little House on the Prairie*.

'Hang on, you hated banana loaf, you said it was a complete humiliation when you found it in your lunch box, Daisy.'

'Yes, it was disgusting, but it was sweet that you made it, it showed that you loved us.'

'And surfing doesn't? Give me that beer.'

I leave them to their nostalgic memories of the earth-mother years and get in the bath.

THE PHILOSOPHY
OF SURF

Woman with three children and 17 Russian hamsters seeks laid-back man with beer and money.

My next potential boyfriend fits the recoupling theory better – he's actually older than me.

The idea of an older man is attractive: someone who could provide the children and me with some stability and order the right wine in restaurants. He would be an experienced lover and have a car that started the first time you turned the key. He wouldn't expect me to watch *Jackass* or read skateboard magazines.

If I was serious about snaring a Silver Surfer, I probably shouldn't have picked a 60-year-old who ran away to Hawaii when he was 16 and spent the rest of his life in search of the Perfect Wave and the perfect beer.

The relationship seemed to be progressing in a slow sort of way, which I put down to our maturity and sophistication, and then he went to California and Mexico and disappeared. He arrived back two months later and we met for a drink, but he had to leave after ten minutes because he received a disturbing text from his son who'd got in a fight, been thrown through a window and needed a lift to casualty.

The next thing I heard he was stuck on a glacier somewhere in Austria. I don't think he was literally clinging on with ice picks, more like stuck in a hotel on a glacier, quite possibly stuck in the bar. As he didn't return my calls for six months I am not sure where he was stuck.

He was so elusive that I began to believe he was a figment of my imagination until I finally bumped into him at Mardi Gras in the next village, a bizarre occasion as they'd decided to kill two birds with one stone and celebrate St Patrick's night at the same time, despite the fact that it was neither Shrove Tuesday nor 17 March. The mix of Irish music and Basque rugby songs was quite moving and the combination of sangria and Guinness surprisingly good.

'Hey, shall we have dinner later?' he asked as if nothing unusual had happened.

I said something along the lines of if I had waited to have dinner with him I might have died of starvation several months ago.

'What's the matter? Are you pissed off just because I didn't return a few calls?' He gets out his phone. 'Look. It's nothing personal, a hundred and twenty-three unanswered messages.'

I tell him 122 are probably from me, but agree to meet him for a drink.

When I arrive at the bar he's looking gloomy.

'What's up?'

'It's my son again.'

'Another fight?'

'No, worse. He wants to get married.'

'Oh, I'm so sorry. Have another beer.'

I can see how this would be worrying. The new man has been married and divorced three times to the same woman. She's the boy's mother, so his son is not genetically predisposed to making a relationship last.

Friends think I should watch out, the Silver Surfer is so hard to pin down he must be commitment-phobic; I however think he's commitmentaholic – only not with me. He went off to discuss the lad's wedding and I haven't seen him since. I guess he got stuck making royal icing.

Oh well, being single means I get to spend more time with my surfboard.

I'm obsessed. I used to think my husband was obsessed. I'd tell him something like: 'I've arranged to see the bank manager at three tomorrow afternoon.'

Nick would look at me as if I was mad. 'Why on earth would you arrange a meeting at *low tide* when there's a westerly swell running?'

He's got me there.

'Because we're a million euros over our overdraft limit and I didn't hear the shipping forecast before the bank manager rang,' I explain patiently.

Now I do exactly the same thing. I hear myself saying, 'No, I can't possibly come into the bank tomorrow morning, I have another rendezvous, but the afternoon would be fine.'

'Monsieur Saint-Cloud is a busy man, couldn't you change the other rendezvous?'

Change the tide? Who does the man think I am, King Canute?

Worse still, I can't remember how to have fun when it's flat.

There's a moment in the English surf movie, *Blue Juice,* when the hero has to decide between getting back in bed with Catherine Zeta-Jones or going surfing. He goes surfing, and the general opinion is: He must be crazy!

He's not crazy – he'll be able to sleep with Catherine when the tide comes in, won't he?

So here I am in the middle of a flat spell, checking the navy charts and trying to remember what I used to do for fun.

Philippe explains it to me. I've been working in the studio all morning and by the time I get into the water there's an onshore gale and the waves are crap. I know the wind always comes up in the afternoon, but I concentrate better in the morning so I feel I ought to put in a few hours before hitting the beach. The Protestant work ethic is a hard habit to kick.

'Wilma,' Philippe sighs, 'you have to understand the philosophy of surf.'

French people love philosophy; any book on philosophy is an instant bestseller, especially when it's author looks like a sexy French movie star.

'What's the philosophy of surf?'

'Simple. When there are waves you surf, when it's flat you work.' Philippe looks like a sexy French movie star; if he could just expand the philosophy beyond a single sentence he'd have a bestseller.

I think about it. It makes a lot of sense and also explains why it's impossible to buy a baguette in the village when there's a swell running.

I think I've become pretty philosophical: it's also hard to get a hot meal at my house when there's a swell running.

BACK TO MY ROOTS

While the Silver Surfer is on a glacier and my other friends are in Bali or Brazil in search of winter sun and tropical waves, I go to London in search of new galleries, new collectors or at the very least a bar that stays open through the winter. The trip also gives me a chance to see my family and to show my kids the culture they've been deprived of: the zoo, the National Gallery, Chinatown and Brent Cross Shopping City.

My parents still live in the house I grew up in on the edge of Highgate Woods in north London, and there's plenty of room for us all to stay. It's always nice to come home to the warmth of the flame-red Aga and the sanctuary of my childhood home.

My upbringing might sound pretty conventional and middle class and in a way it was – leafy suburbs, hothouse girls' school, piano lessons and ballet classes, brown Labrador and a Volvo estate car. But my parents are slightly eccentric and the house is not so much a conventional suburban home as a surreal museum.

Nothing has ever been thrown away. When I go back I can find anything: my old school uniform, the outfit I wore to a

Clash concert in 1977, primary school macaroni paintings, an attic full of oil paintings, a Neo Naturist movie made in body paint in the snow in their garden. In my bedroom there's a glass case full of lumps of lava that I brought back from Iceland and fossils from the Lyme Regis mud, and on the chest of drawers a strange arrangement of my Barbie dolls with cropped hair and missing limbs, the Victorian china doll I bought in an antique shop in 1969 and a doll with real fingernails my grandparents brought me back from Brazil. There are odd socks dating back to 1972 – proof of my mother's eternal optimism: her belief that the matching socks will turn up.

It's not just my stuff that has been kept. An archaeologist could write the family history from the things in the house: spinning wheels and riding clothes from my mother's spinster aunts from Buckinghamshire; 1930s cocktail dresses and African masks from a globe-trotting aunt from Philadelphia; my father's wooden rocking horse; the eighteenth-century marble fireplace my mother saved from a skip in Hampstead.

My father had a high-powered job in the city but he'd originally wanted to be an artist and used to live in a bohemian artists' studio in Hammersmith, and this was the side of him we always saw. He would wander round the house in a kimono at weekends singing along to the soundtrack of *The Jungle Book* with us and cooking ratatouille, roast garlic and coq au vin. His recipes were very avant-garde for the 1960s and sometimes caused me severe embarrassment when school friends came round expecting fish fingers. From time to time he would disappear to the other side of the world on business trips, returning home with flickering cine film of faraway lands and gifts of kimonos from Japan, Arab robes from Saudi Arabia, shot silk from Hong Kong or scarab necklaces from Egypt. I think these gifts sparked my desire to travel, along with his stories of hitch-hiking round Europe with a suit in his rucksack. I followed in his footsteps later with New Romantic party dresses in my rucksack.

I think my mother should have been an artist too. Nick used to describe her as 'the last of the surrealists'. She had four children and worked part time as a teacher, but still seemed to be overflowing with energy. Mum doesn't like to stay still and always has a new project on the go. While my father cooked, she would have a vat of lichen or onion skins on the other hob in which she would dye sheep's wool to spin on her aunts' spinning wheel and then knit jumpers for the whole family. Or she might be carving driftwood sculptures, planting trees in the garden, making patchwork quilts or sewing flamboyant evening dresses out of Liberty prints in which to play the corporate wife. She loves clothes and taught us from an early age never to worry what other people thought of us and to dress exactly as we wanted.

There was a time, when I was trying to fit in with my school friends, that I aspired to normality and wished my parents would buy their clothes from Marks & Spencer and behave like families in sitcoms. I had got over this by the time I was 17 and became a punk.

When the school rang to complain that I'd dyed my hair green, my mother's reaction was typical, 'What's the problem, don't you think it suits her complexion?'

I was particularly embarrassed by my father's absent-minded professor look. He wore thick tortoiseshell glasses, had wild black hair and was so tall his jeans never reached his socks. None of this ever bothered him, but it forced me to make him wait around the corner when he picked me up from parties. So I was surprised when I went to art college and found that my friends adored Dad's geek style. They were also very charmed by his habit of opening the door with the greeting: 'Are you staying for lunch? Would you like a dry martini?'

It was the ideal home in which to play dressing up, both as a child and as an art student. It was like a theatrical costume house with the family's vintage clothes going back to the turn of the twentieth century. When I was ten I dressed as Calamity Jane for a whole year. In the 1980s my great-grandmother's bed jacket made the tour of Soho clubs and bars, along with my grandmother's 1930s ski pants and the jeans my mother wore for a road trip across America in 1956.

Nothing has changed except that it is my daughters who rummage through the wardrobes and attic, and I'm rather alarmed to find that my own old clothes are classed as vintage, classic 1980s retro. My father is still there to welcome me with the cocktail shaker and my mother with some weird and wonderful gift she's made: a mohair blanket, an après-surf towelling poncho or a jumper for my dog.

My business trips to London are usually to sell paintings, attend exhibitions or receive commissions, which are going along nicely, but I felt as if my career was on a bit of a plateau until one spring morning in Olatua.

I opened my email and found one saying that the Mamas Surf Club would meet at two and that we should bring beer and sausages to the beach. The next was an invitation to a show at a major London art museum – the Institute of Contemporary Art (ICA). The exhibition was a collection of subversive art movements from the 1980s, titled 'The Secret Public: The Last Days of the British Underground', and featured the Neo Naturists.

Hang on – that's ME!

I started the Neo Naturists with my friends Jennifer and Christine Binnie when I was at art college. Christine came to college as a life model; she was bored of posing and I was bored of life drawing, so we came up with a more interesting plan. Jennifer was studying painting at Portsmouth and living with Grayson Perry, who became the fourth member of the group. We did live art performances wearing nothing but body paint and patchouli.

Our philosophy was best summed up by Marlon Brando in *The Wild One*, when someone asked Brando's character, 'What are you rebelling against?' and he answered: 'What've you got?'

We performed at nightclubs, art galleries, festivals, the British Museum and even in the street. The highlight of my career was my debut – too early to say for sure but probably also my final appearance – at the Royal Opera House, which was the realisation of a childhood ambition. As an eight year old hooked on *Ballet Shoes* I probably imagined I would be wearing a tutu and pirouetting into Rudolf Nureyev's arms, rather than cheerleading naked. But that's another story.

I am delighted to finally be showing in such a prestigious gallery. I admit that I'd rather be showing my latest masterpieces, still dripping with paint in my basement studio, than work I did 20 years ago. But I'm not going to complain about being invited to a VIP champagne reception in a major art museum and having my work described as: 'A dark flowering of creativity, with a backdrop of civil unrest in Thatcherite Britain.' Hell, I'm not just an art star, I'm a fucking hero of the revolution with a bit of Yoko Ono thrown in. What to tell my surf buddies? This bit of my past has never cropped up in après-surf conversation, and there is a risk they'll think me a little strange – or totally nuts.

Then there are the kids, how are they going to react?

I bite the bullet when I find a photo from the show on the Internet.

'Hey, Nat, do you want to see this? It's performance art, a bit like that theatre class you did in St-Jean-de-Luz.' Not too much like it, I hope, but he's a teenage skateboarder and he might need a reference point.

He looks at the invite, then at me and raises an eyebrow.

'You know, Nat, you have to put it in the context of challenging body stereotypes and the cult of anorexia in the fashion world during the 1980s. And, er… ' I'm using the gallery press release for inspiration, '… it was the last outburst of radical experimentation before the onslaught of consumerism.'

'Oh, so you're not a stripper then?' he says with very little conviction.

Didn't they teach him anything in that drama class? Despite the comments, my kids are delighted. Because, now, whenever they get in trouble for leaving turtles in the kitchen sink, dyeing their hair pink, letting off firecrackers or melting leg-wax over the oven, they can turn round and say, 'Well, at least *we've* never been arrested for walking around the streets of London NAKED!'

With hindsight I should have left that particular photo out of the album. They fall about laughing as I try to point out that we were not, technically speaking, being arrested. The nice young policeman in the fountains at Centre Point was simply telling us that if we did not put our clothes on he would be obliged to arrest us. There is a difference, but I guess it doesn't make me Mama Walton.

In the end, my ego gets the better of me and I tell everyone when I read a review describing the Neo Naturists as 'the forgotten but brilliant last subcultural art movement'.

It's a rather surreal experience flying over for the reception and seeing the display of photos, drawings and tubs of body paint in a glass case, rather like a museum vitrine showing relics of a lost civilisation. In the centre of the display is a photo showing what appears to be a group of cavewomen, smeared in swirls of black body paint gathered round a bonfire gnawing on charred bones. They look like a lost tribe rediscovered by *National Geographic*. It takes me a while to realise that the woman in the centre of the group is me. It was taken during a week-long live-in event in Wapping, and we're on the banks of the River Thames.

Maybe not that much has changed after all: a group of women round a fire eating spare ribs and drinking beer, having a laugh and trying to smash a few stereotypes along the way.

If you swap the black body paint for black neoprene and Wapping for Olatua, it could be the Mamas Surf Club.

Following the show, Christine Binnie puts together an archive of Neo Naturist memorabilia that the Tate shows an interest in acquiring – every artist's dream. I go into my mother's attic and find some cabaret props – a moulting feather boa, some wigs, a pair of gold platform mules, a sequinned bra and a lilac corset from the 1950s.

I meet Christine in a bar to donate the trophies and we toast our rather belated recognition by the art world with a pint of cider.

Thirty years of struggle in the art world, and finally the Tate wants my old underwear.

LADIES WHO DON'T LUNCH

Back home the Surf Mamas are gaining confidence. When the weather is warm and the waves are small, we start going out alone and with the extra practice, we improve quickly.

At the weekends we take our kids to the beach, if we can persuade them to go, but sometimes the Mamas sneak off while the kids are at school. There's something very liberating about heading off on a weekday, like skiving school. My partners in crime are usually Jo, Taryn and Florence.

Florence and I are both single now and work freelance, which is very useful in the quest for the Perfect Wave.

Jo isn't getting on well with her husband and he's lost enthusiasm for her new hobby although he surfs himself – or perhaps it is *because* he surfs? Jo works with her husband in their street fashion brand he designs, and sometimes she hides her board and sneaks out of the house pretending she's going to the office. On the way home from the beach, she'll stop at mine to dry her hair.

Taryn's husband Steve is very supportive, he loves her going surfing and rings from work sometimes to say, 'Stop what you're doing – you and Wilma should go to the naturist beach and catch some waves right now.' Apart from running a skateboard company, Steve has started producing a brand of rosé called Couer Clementine, which becomes the official beverage of the surf club.

We surf perfect waves on beautiful sunny days when Olatua looks like a photo in a luxury travel brochure. We also surf imperfect waves and total junk if we're desperate enough.

We choose a beach between Biarritz and the border based on swell conditions, wind direction, how much time we have and how brave we're feeling.

For a long time we head to Hendaye even if it's almost flat, and then one day we reach a turning point.

'Do you think the wave's a bit... small?'

'Never too small for the Mamas.'

'I don't know – there are limits. Shall we go back up the coast and find some bigger waves?'

When I lived with a surfer and didn't surf, I used to think all this driving was a total waste of time and petrol. As Robert Louis Stevenson said, 'to travel hopefully is a better thing than to arrive'. Half the fun is cruising along the coast, stopping at beaches, grabbing an ice cream or churros depending on the season and then getting back in the car, driving round the corniche to St-Jean-de-Luz, paddling out in to the bay, watching the sun go down over the ocean and arriving in Olatua in time for a beer on the beach at twilight.

It's fun cruising around pretending to be in a teenage road movie, talking about waves and boys, listening to country-and-western music. It's also fun pulling up at a break with the boards piled on the roof and seeing the reaction when a group of forty-something women get out of the car. It's a satisfying feeling surprising passers-by and other surfers, who often do a double take and look around for another car full of men. We're certainly not a classic group of surf bunnies, but we're not a bunch of middle-aged frumps in twin sets either.

Taryn's look is Western cowboy chic with ten years in Paris thrown in: cowboy boots or wooden platform sandals, a cocktail dress, a Levi's jacket, a bit of Navajo jewellery. Jo is the English rose, blonde and blue eyed, who wears white linen, florals and baby pink flip-flops that match her lip gloss. Flo has a mane of auburn hair and effortless Parisian style, and can even make a boiler suit look sexy if she's come straight from work. My look goes from bohemian artist to grunge revival, depending on whether I've had time to change or come straight from the studio, in which case I'm usually covered in paint and a dusting of glitter, my hair pinned up with a paintbrush or a pencil.

One day I'm with Taryn in Hendaye and a wonderful thing happens.

We're sitting out there pretty much alone when another surfer joins us. A set comes in and we back off saying, 'No really your wave, please take it.'

We're assuming he's a local, a real surfer who somehow has more right to the wave because he's a man in a man's world. He takes a wave and Taryn and I look at each other in disbelief.

'Did you see that?'

'That was amazing!'

What happened might not seem amazing or inspiring to anyone else, but to us it was the best. The man gets the wave, tries to stand up and falls into the water with a big splash.

'Am I imagining it or is that guy a worse surfer than us?'

We don't mean it personally, he seems nice enough, he's just a beginner who probably thought it will be less threatening to practise on this little wave with a couple of middle-aged women than among a lot of macho men.

He made our day. We are no longer the worst surfers in the line-up. You can't blame us for feeling pretty good about that!

I am no longer officially 'the worst surfer in the world'. Maybe it's time to surf the wave of my dreams...

THE LINE-UP

The wave I've always dreamed of surfing is the one that broke outside our window when we first moved to Olatua. The wave picks up the biggest swell and breaks way out, rolling in across the bay, so it's not a beginner's wave; it's one of those famous waves that people travel from all over the world to surf.

I'm sure that there's no such thing as an ugly wave, but this is a particularly beautiful, perfectly formed one with curves in all the right places, which breaks over a submerged reef in the middle of a smooth calm ocean. I've seen it breaking 10-metres high, but a few days later it will be glassy calm. I'm looking for something in between. As you set off from shore it's like a little sea voyage, you're wondering what the wave will look like up close.

Although I can surf now, the last 500 metres out to the Olatua wave is one of the hardest parts of my journey. It takes me a long time to get the guts to paddle out there, and even longer to do it alone. I feel sick, full of butterflies. Not only that, but with the beach and bars all facing the wave it's like an amphitheatre, and it's sod's law that no one will see your waves, but they will all catch your wipeouts.

I know that really deep water is safer than shallow water, as long as you can swim. However hard you hit it, water makes a softer landing than rocks, coral, sand or children playing in the shore break. I've had my worst injuries in knee-deep water: broken collarbone and toes, head-to-toe bruises, black eyes and nosebleeds, and then there were the times in the shallows when I stood on a weaver fish and had a jellyfish sting on my chin that made me look like Alfred Hitchcock. (The lifeguards helpfully suggested peeing on it. I do a lot of yoga, but have you ever tried peeing on your own chin?)

But even knowing that deep is safer than shallow there is the *Jaws* paranoia, the collective subconscious fear of Davy Jones's Locker full of sea witches and whale graveyards, and the knowledge that however much we want to be mermaids we can't breathe underwater. The deep is still the deep.

Even more intimidating is the line-up, the place where surfers sit on their boards and wait for the wave. You can't just take a wave anywhere, there's a right and a wrong place to sit; if you're in the wrong place you won't get a wave or it will break right over your head. So everyone sits together in a line, jostling for position. You can imagine how it feels paddling into the middle of a group of tough athletic men who have been surfing for 20 years longer than you and saying, 'Move over, boys, this wave is mine.'

Before you get in the water, there's the walk down the beach kissing anyone you pass on both cheeks. There's a bit of small talk; if you're talking to a surfer it will be a fascinating, life-changing piece of information like, 'The swell's picking up at the weekend and the wind will be offshore all day.'

For non-surfers, small talk is more trivial: 'Nice weather', 'I just left my husband' or 'A giant meteorite is about to hit earth'.

I don't run down the beach. It's a pose and also I don't want to exhaust myself before I get wet. I'm more likely to run back up the beach afterwards when I'm late for the school run or in dire need of a hot bath or a cold beer.

The next bit is paddling across the lagoon avoiding kids on lilos, floating movie stars and Spanish men with harpoon guns and dead octopuses.

Once you cross the reef, the fun begins.

You've done the easy bit: you've negotiated the ocean currents and submerged rocks, the odd Portuguese man-of-war, oil slick or cocaine dump. On a crowded day the line-up can be a bit like an offshore dinner party, you have to choose who to sit next to. The difference is that if you sit next to the wrong person you might suffer serious injury to yourself, your board or your ego.

It works more or less like this: men on the bigger waves, which break furthest out; women and children nearer the shore on the smaller, less scary waves. There are exceptions but, as in strict Muslim countries and on couples' cycling holidays, the woman is usually trailing 20 metres behind.

If it *were* a party, my natural inclination would be to go way out there to the VIP lounge and join the local hard core surfers, who are friends of mine – people I would be perfectly happy to chat to on the beach. But I'm not ready to surf alongside them yet, so I end up gatecrashing the kids' tea party inshore. This would be OK and bearable if I was able to show them a few tricks and give them the benefit of my superior wisdom. Sadly a lot of them are better at surfing than me, or they're only inside on the smaller waves because they have shorter boards and they're five years old.

One day a disturbing incident convinces me that it's time to move a bit further out and take my chances with the big boys.

A man I've never seen before paddles out with his son. The poor boy looks green around the gills as if he'd rather be back on the beach eating ice cream and building sandcastles with *maman* than having this macho male-bonding moment with *papa*.

Then *papa* says, 'Stay in here with this woman. She'll look after you.'

I can't believe it. He doesn't ask me, 'Is this the offshore crèche facility?' or say, 'I'd like to recouple with you, let's start the shared childcare right away.' He doesn't even say, '*Bonjour*.' He just paddles off towards the horizon, naively assuming that he can rely on my maternal instincts to make sure his son doesn't drown. What he hasn't put into his equation is that if I were the maternal sort, I might have stayed home and made my own children lunch instead of telling them to microwave some popcorn to take the edge off their appetites until the wind goes onshore and I get out of the water.

I don't like to see the boy's face frozen in fear, so I tell him to watch out for big sets and I head out to sea without looking back. I know he's not really in danger, but I know how he feels only too well and I don't bother to tell him, 'It's only water.'

217

On my way out I pass Alain Gardinier, a suave writer and film-maker about my age. He's a way better surfer than me, but I can tell by his attitude that it's not a scary day. He looks very relaxed and smiles as he surfs past. Nothing particularly unusual about it except that he's standing on his head.

When I get out there I take the Zen approach. I sit a little apart from the crowd and think that if a wave is part of my destiny it will come my way; if not, I'll just sit here and admire the view. Sometimes all you need to raise your game is a bit of attitude. The man dumping his son was the first attitude booster; the dentist was the next.

I'm sitting out on the peak, it's crowded and I'm vaguely wishing there was another woman out here to bond with because I'm drowning in testosterone. On the one hand, I have something to prove for womankind; on the other hand, am I the right woman for the job?

Then a dentist gives me a slightly snotty look.

I don't know why the fact that he's a dentist should wind me up. Some of my best friends are dentists, my grandmother was one of the first women dentists in the 1920s, and without dentists I would be a toothless crone. So, any dentists reading this, believe me, I love you all, it's just that this guy's not a Hawaiian lifeguard or anything, which immediately makes me think if a dentist can take these waves so can I.

I catch a look in the dentist's eye that seems to say: Shouldn't you be on the smaller waves on the inside, or further in on the sand or better still in the kitchen preparing foie gras? He's probably not thinking that at all, he's more likely dreaming about some new root-canal technique, a nice Audi coupé he saw in the showroom or how pretty the sunshine looks sparkling on the water like gold fillings. He may even be thinking: Why is Wilma giving me such a funny look?

But the look is enough to inspire me to paddle further over and further out and take a wave.

Lots of things can go wrong when you surf, but there are also a lot of things that can go right. On this day the wave decides to do me a favour. It picks me up and carries me in towards the beach, rolling out a wall of shimmering water in front of me like a red carpet. I see people lying in the water below me, but I know I'm not going to hit them because I can effortlessly flick the nose of the board out of their way. When I've finished, I lie in the water laughing and thinking: I am completely awesome.

A complete stranger paddles past and says, *'Belle vague!'*

As he gets closer, he looks surprised then impressed to see that I'm an older woman and I think for a moment he might be about to add, *'Belle vague, madame.'*

After all the times I've hoped no one was watching, it's lovely to be thinking: I hope *everyone* was watching!

I don't like to leave it hanging in the air, so I go into the Bahia beach bar and interrupt everyone's lunch.

'Hey, did you see that wave?' What I mean is, I hope you weren't all sitting there looking at your food.

François Lartigau is there, he's an artist, a surfer and a traveller, very core and very cool. It's hard to believe he's been surfing these waves since the 1960s. He's a 60-year-old man trapped in the body of a 40-year-old board-short model.

He says, 'Yes, I saw it, it was fantastic, Wilma. I'm proud of you. I remember when you started and I honestly never thought you'd do that. You're a real surfer now!'

Real Surfer. I want to have it tattooed on my arm.

I keep smiling for the rest of the day and kiss everyone I see.

Part
Four

BIARRITZ AND THE FRENCH DESERT

Alongside the search for the Perfect Wave and the perfect man, there's always the search for the perfect gallery. I still imagine mine is in New York, Los Angeles or Shanghai, but things don't always happen as you expect.

I've been working in the studio during the winter. Although I surf throughout the year there is less temptation in winter, and certainly less temptation to hang out on the beach afterwards drinking rosé and waiting for the elusive green flash at sunset. This phenomenon is meant to be quite amazing, like the Northern Lights, an explosion of light across the horizon just after the sun sets. But the conditions have to be perfect and the more I talk to people about it, the more I think that the perfect conditions include being completely stoned.

I've enjoyed my studio time, but I do need to get out of Olatua from time to time, so when I got an invitation on Facebook to a private view and Burns Night dinner in the Limousin I jumped at the chance. I only knew my host in an ethereal way and, like most artists, I love a good private view and I hadn't eaten haggis for a while. It was a long way to go for a free glass of wine, but the five-hour drive was worth it for the surreal experience of finding a cutting-edge contemporary art gallery in the middle of nowhere, complete with an exact replica of the Colony Room, the infamous Soho drinking club that was a second home to artists from Francis Bacon to Damien Hirst and me. I took the children out of school for a couple of days, putting 'Cultural excursion' as the reason for absence.

For someone who has technically lived in France for so long, I've seen surprisingly little of the country. This is partly because I don't really live in France at all but the Pays Basque. You're in a different country once you cross the River Adour in Bayonne and head into the flat piney forest of Les Landes. Inland are reclaimed swamplands, foie gras ducks and wooden farmhouses; on the coast is the hard core surf community in Hossegor. Pro surfers in the tubes, their wives back home fattening ducks, cooling beer and looking hot in their teeny weeny polka dot bikinis.

My instructions were to turn left at Bordeaux, and once we got past the St-Émilion vineyards we were in the French desert.

It isn't desert as in sand dunes, Bedouin tribesmen, camels and oil sheikhs in 4 x 4s. Despite the Saharan temperature inside the car. It's desert as in deserted. The expression came from a book called *Paris and the French Desert,* published in 1947, and despite global over-population in the last 60 years nothing much has changed. In the 300 kilometres between Bordeaux and our first stopover in the Limousin we only saw about ten people, mostly old men in berets with wooden sticks, who were probably there when the book was written and looked as if they hadn't changed clothes since. The towns were like ghost towns with faded Cinzano ads painted on crumbling walls, a church, a cemetery and maybe an old Michelin garage with rusting petrol pumps in the forecourt: you could see that the petrol had dried up long ago. In some places there were skull-and-crossbone flags hanging at the entrance to town with *'Village en Danger de Mort'* written on them. Occasionally we saw a tractor in a field of haystacks, presumably driven by a living human being, but apart from that it was like the Empty Quarter. There are towns out here that the French government will pay you to live in.

After three hours on empty B-roads we came to a village full of concrete sheep.

Nat, who has never been a big fan of rural wilderness, laughed. 'Oh my God, the last thing they need here is concrete sheep, why didn't they make some concrete people instead? When are we going to get to this place anyway?'

'We're only five minutes away,' I say.

It should be right here. I love mappy.com, but I thought it had fucked up this time as we pulled up outside an ancient-looking tractor shop with faded posters of rural man's dream machines in the window.

'Over there, maybe.' Alice pointed across the road.

And there it was, in the centre of Magnac-Laval, the Galerie Planet, an oasis of decadence in the French desert.

A handsome Sikh from Hackney was painting calligraphy in gold leaf onto a topless woman's back, a mix of local and international artists, farmers and ex-pats were drinking champagne, and the back room had been converted into a faithful replica of the Colony Room. The walls were the exact same viridian green, and hung with work by YBA art stars like Damien Hirst and Tracey Emin; the only unauthentic touch was the quality of the wine, which was way too good, but I didn't let this get to me. This was an interesting alternative to moving to the place where your favourite bar is – you move the bar to the place where you live.

James Anderson is a suave and charming Scottish aristocrat who had a vision of bringing serious art and Soho-style drinking to the Limousin. It's hard to tell what made him give up the bright lights of London town and set up his gallery in a village with one street and no streetlights. I suppose I should understand having made a similar move myself, but at least my village has a few more restaurants and bars, but the fact that they're all closed is part of the reason that I've driven over 400 kilometres for a drink and a conversation with someone I'm not related to.

At the private view talk shifts between John Beazley's pop-art-revisited paintings and the superior texture and taste of Limousin beef. A man I meet at the afters party in the 'Colony Room' offers me a ride in his eight-wheeler.

'Oh,' I say politely, 'is that a tractor?'

He looks at me as if I'm crazy. Apparently tractors don't have eight wheels – worth remembering if you're trying to pick up a farmer.

'No, of course not, it's an ex-army *véhicule*.'

There's an awkward silence. He's wondering how anyone could reach my age without knowing how many wheels a tractor has, and I'm wondering why anyone would ask you to go cruising in a tank.

The next morning it's as if the private view never happened; the streets are empty again – or maybe I should say the street is empty as there is only the one – except for an old man with a baguette staring dreamily into the window of the tractor shop. We have a day to kill before the Burns Night dinner, so the kids and I explore. We find an estate agent and I start laughing. 'Look at these prices.'

The kids are not experts on real estate, but they get the joke. You could buy the whole village for the price of a house with a sea view in Biarritz. This is the sort of place English people come to live the dream, buy a huge chateau, plant a vineyard, start a llama farm, retire early to a life of fine wine and runny cheese.

There's an English tea house called Vettriano's where you can read *The Telegraph* under a print of *The Singing Butler*. And there's an ex-pat food aisle in the supermarket that the kids take full advantage of, making the most of my hangover and some imaginary guilt complex they think I should have about bringing them up in Biarritz.

'Oooh, English sweets. We've never lived in our birthplace, we've missed out on so much of our heritage... and this *is* a cultural excursion, isn't it?'

The trolley is quickly loaded up with salt and vinegar crisps, Crunchie bars, Cadbury's Creme Eggs. I get a little carried away with the nostalgia for the Old Country myself and fill another basket with gourmet delights unavailable in the Pays Basque. Luckily I take another look before I reach the checkout: Bird's Custard powder, pre-packed Cheddar, baked beans, *mushy peas*.

I've never bought this stuff in my life, why start now when I live in a country where food is the religion? I leave it all at the till except the kid's junk and a bottle of Lucozade, which I keep for medicinal purposes.

If I had thought Magnac-Laval was the middle of nowhere, I wasn't prepared for the next stop. James's house, where the Burns Night party is being held, is up a dead-end farm track in a hamlet where the streets have no names.

On the way we cruise along roads empty from one horizon to the other, past deserted market towns and meadows, ducks swimming in rivers with laundry stones on the banks, avenues of elm trees. It's hard to know if we're more likely to see another car or a horse and cart. There are menhirs in the fields and huge cathedrals in empty villages, built by returning crusaders in honour of God and chastity belts. It's like going back in time 200 years.

It's dark and misty by the time we find James's place, like walking into *Brigadoon*. James is a perfect host, he's in a kilt and sporran, playing the grand piano under a stag's head. Portraits of the Anderson clan look down from the walls, candles flicker in ornate silver candlesticks and the smell of haggis wafts from the kitchen. The other guests are mostly artists and writers, including the Sikh artist who proves a big hit with Alice and Nat when he takes off his turban and unravels his knee-length hair for them. There's also the local beekeeper with a waist-length beard like a Druid, who lives with his family in a hut in the woods with no electricity, and his children have the highest grades in the school.

'*Fromage!*' shouts the beekeeper every time we make a toast – his translation of 'cheers', which he hears as 'cheese'. The toasts go on until five in the morning by which time I've become quite attached to the Limousin and have suggested myself as artist-in-residence to Magnac-Laval.

I think about it on the way home the next day. I could have a huge studio and devote myself to my work. The kids could hang out with the beekeeper's daughters, I could drive round the countryside in a tank, drink Tetley's tea in Vettriano's and vodka tonic in the 'Colony Room' with James. And after all, Paris is only two hours away.

I'm not sure what I'd paint; the whole place is like an eighteenth-century painting, even the trees look somehow old-fashioned. Maybe I could change my style to romantic landscapes? It would be a bit of a *volte-face*, I admit.

When we get home after another six hours in the car, the air is warm and salty. I can hear the waves from the motorway exit in Biarritz. It's midwinter, but it's balmy T-shirt weather in the afternoon sunshine. There's a 4-metre swell and no wind; it's perfect glassy surf; the beach is packed with surfers, spectators and photographers; there are big-wave heroes and bongo drums; and broken boards, smashed in two by the force of the waves in heavy wipeouts.

Johanna has just had her baby, François tells me, a little girl called Lina. It was a tough birth, but they're both fine.

'Great! When was she born?' The Mamas Surf Club had been anxiously waiting for Johanna to become a mama.

'About fifteen minutes ago.'

'Wow, that's so sweet. Christophe rang to tell you?'

Laughter. 'No, he was ringing to see what the waves were like. It's the best swell this winter – he rang five times while she was in labour!'

It's nice to be home. I can't go and live in the desert, I'm a surfer.

SEX AND DRUGS
AND BABY WIPES

It's a bit of a shock to see how small Lina is. I still think of Alice as pretty much new-born and she's just gone to secondary school.

It's nice to be able to give younger friends the benefit of my ten years as an earth mother, especially when they know so much more about press-ups and take-offs and cut-backs than you. I feel like at last I have something to give back, but I do sometimes wonder about the pearls of maternal wisdom I'm sharing: the first six months are the hardest. What am I talking about? That's up there with childbirth doesn't hurt, you won't go off sex and your jeans will still fit you.

We all try to convince ourselves that life will be so much easier once the kid is crawling, walking, weaned or potty-trained. But then they're out of nappies and next thing you know they're wearing thongs and you have a whole heap of more complex childcare issues to worry about – like sex and drugs and rock 'n' roll.

Then you have to decide where you stand on this. Do you tell them you met their dad at a Salvation Army cake sale? Or tell them the truth but insist they don't do as you have done. Trust me, I tried it, and look what it got me: three children, a hangover and 24 hours of Bruce Springsteen on my iPod.

How do you simultaneously maintain your authority and your coolness?

I worry about drugs. I've taken the precaution of bringing them to live far away from the big city to a sleepy little Basque fishing village. Actually, after the Limousin it doesn't seem so sleepy, it just suffers from mood swings, shifting from catatonic to frenzied season by season. One thing I didn't take into account was the fact that apart from being on the 'Route des Fromages', Olatua is also on the 'Route de Cocaine' between South America and the rest of Europe. It's better to dump it than get caught with it. Drug traffickers dump so much coke in the Bay of Biscay you could develop a habit just by breathing through your nose when you swim front crawl. When we arrived the beaches were awash with it, and it was so cheap that the tramps in Bayonne were selling it to pay for their rosé, which ended badly for them when the Colombians came to get it back, 'Oh sorry, I sold it. Would you like a glass of rosé?'

From time to time paranoia sets in. I find a blue pill on my daughter's bedroom floor while I'm hoovering. I guess I'm a bit bored or I wouldn't be hoovering. I panic: what is it? I know nothing about drugs. For me to recognise it, it would have to be labelled with letters big enough to focus on without my reading glasses. I toy with the idea of eating it to see what happens, but this seems a risky strategy. So I decide to cut it in half, a fairly futile gesture with my limited knowledge of designer drugs of the twenty-first century, and see what's inside. As it turns out this is one banned substance I do know. It's a blue Smartie.

Technically speaking, the ban I imposed on blue Smarties when the children were younger has never been lifted, so I could give her a hard time. Oh, no, I couldn't, because she clearly hasn't eaten it.

But there is an even more worrying prospect than your kids going wild: your kids not going wild.

A few days later I'm sorting though the junk in my basement.

'No one minds if I give the baby Lego to little Lina do they?'

'Oh no, you can't give my Duplo zoo away!' Daisy is mortified.

I feel a little black thundercloud forming over my head.

'Why not?' I ask suspiciously.

If there's one thing more scary than the idea of them going wild, it's the idea of them settling down, being sensible, getting a mortgage, getting married and making me a GRANDMOTHER. Total paranoia of course, it is just a vision of the future when the Mamas Surf Club might become the Nanas Surf Club after all.

OK, they're only 17, 14 and 11, but I see the nightmare scenario looming somewhere down the road. I went to a party recently hosted by a French woman my age about to become a *mamie* – she insisted all night she really didn't mind; the leather jeans, thigh length boots and sequinned belly top were saying something very different. I had the decency to wait until my mother was 65 before I provided her with her first grandchild, but even so she didn't consider herself old enough.

'I don't think it would be appropriate for her to call me Granny,' said my mum. Why on earth not? In the end I comforted her with the thought that Daisy wouldn't actually be able to talk when she was born, so she would have a couple of years to get used to the idea of being called Granny.

Then I remember my own grandmother, the matriarch in Lyme Regis, and that cheers me up a lot. She was a great inspiration to me, I adored her and I dread to think what she would have done to me if I'd called her Granny. Her real name was Iris, but she wouldn't stand for that either – she told me she was bored of the purple flowers by the time she was 20 because she had so many admirers, but the irises kept coming for the next 80 years. We called her Idy. She lived until she was 100 sustained on a diet of Cheddar cheese, water biscuits, weak tea and strong gin and tonic. It was only in her nineties that she would occasionally refuse her cocktail hour G&T in favour of a margarita, a drink I introduced her to when she was 95.

Daisy is persuaded and we hand over a bag of toys to Johanna. Watching her with little Lina makes me wonder how I ever did it. It's one of the things in my life I look back on with awe. It's astonishing the kids even survived: the blue Smartie incident was nothing compared to the evening Daisy came toddling down from my mother's attic with a bag of mothballs in her hand saying, 'Granny Annie's sweeties yucky.' (No, my mother didn't escape the granny label; with a name like Annie she didn't stand a chance.)

Twelve hours in emergency and the next weekend she ate a sleeping pill. It's definitely easier now.

It's better when your kids are old enough to wash themselves, microwave their own popcorn and drink beer; it's also a shock when your babies are no longer babies. They spring things on you like, 'Mum, I'm going to live in Paris.'

'What? Without me?' was my not wholly coherent response.

'Er… yes, sorry.' I can see that it wouldn't be entirely appropriate for Daisy to take me with her when she leaves home, especially as she's going to live with her father's new fiancée.

The news that she's going was mostly a big relief; the school wasn't too keen to keep her and we're running out of choices locally.

I've recently had to sign a letter from the school accepting a specific dress code agreement for her – one clause states that she cannot wear *décolleté* AND a short skirt at the same time. One or the other will be acceptable.

She treats this with the disdain it deserves. 'As if I would wear a mini skirt with a low cut top, what do they think I am, a hooker?'

I understand the problem one day when I drop her off at school. She's wearing a vintage, slightly shredded 1950s dress from my mother's attic, probably once worn by my respectable great aunts, but paired with platforms, laddered tights, a peroxide beehive and full stage make-up, the dress has a whole new life. To me this seems like an entirely normal way to dress when you're 17, but looking around I realise that every other girl in the school has long, glossy, natural-coloured hair and is wearing jeans, a designer anorak and flat *ballerines* or Converse. It looks like the casting session for a hair conditioner or a low fat yoghurt ad. Daisy looks like she escaped from the set of a 1960s art house movie or an ad for Smirnoff.

She might have been able to get away with her eccentric attire, and her grades fluctuating between inconsistent and consistently bad with occasional flashes of brilliance, but her pathological lateness seals her fate. She's late every day for a year, the excuses wear thin.

But there is one day of the year when everyone loves her – the day of the school show. The same teachers who politely requested that she change school still talk in awed tones about her angelic singing voice, rock diva attitude and general star quality.

She performs everything from 'Whiskey in the Jar' to 'Non, Je Ne Regrette Rien'.

But the blow is softened knowing I'm doing the right thing, and Daisy's new school – Lycée Edgar Poe – sounds perfect. (Edgar Allan Poe is a cult writer in France, partly because Baudelaire translated his work.) I somehow just know it's going to suit her.

It's A Moment when fledglings abandon the nest, leaving sad old mummies alone with their memories and their rescue cats. (I had adopted an abandoned kitten from the RSPCA and it promptly abused my hospitality by getting pregnant and having five more kittens.)

'I won't change a thing in your room, darling.'

'You can hoover it and change the sheets if you want.'

I know it's the way of the world and I've been prepared for it for a while. I can remember the first conversation I ever had about Daisy leaving home.

'The important thing about children is to let them go. Don't forget, when the time comes they have to live their own lives,' this woman told me. I saw her point, but I thought it was a little bit early to bring it up. I was six months' pregnant and she was my midwife. I felt like crying. For God's sake, she's not even born, she hasn't got eyelashes, I can't let her out into the big wide world yet.

Now Daisy has eyelashes to spare and she's not just leaving me, she's going to Paris.

I have a troubled relationship with Paris. I know it's a wonderful city full of art, love and *haute couture*, but I find it deeply intimidating. This goes back to my childhood. My mother is in many ways a very open-minded person, but there are certain things of which she disapproves, and we were brought up to treat these things with suspicion. Among the suspicious items were: pistachio ice cream, Enid Blyton books, very handsome men and Paris. I got over my prejudice against very handsome men and green ice cream, but I never read Daisy *Noddy Goes to Toyland* or felt at home in the French capital.

When I was a baby my father was a foreign correspondent and we lived in Paris for three years. My mother didn't like it much. She never forgave the Parisians for not letting her breastfeed me at the top of the Eiffel Tower. I was probably as upset as she was at the time, and I think the experience might have left emotional scars.

Then I was sent there to stay in a student hostel for a few weeks when I was 17 to improve my French A-level prospects. It was 1977 and I had just discovered punk – and Paris had not.

I was dressed head to toe in leopard skin with black eyeshadow, purple lipstick and peroxide-blonde hair. Men drew their own conclusions, and I think the only phrase I really mastered in French was: 'No, *monsieur*, I am *not* a prostitute. I am, for your information, a *punquette*.'

Later, when I was at art college, it was the last stop-off point on hitch-hiking trips round Italy. My friend Mo had a hospitable friend in Paris who would put us up and give us luncheon vouchers. By the time we got there we'd be broke; my boho chic would have deteriorated into hobo chic. My look was, once again, a little too *avant-garde*. *Le Grunge* would appear on the catwalks ten years later, but like many visionaries, I was misunderstood and ridiculed.

Nothing much has changed. I think I look OK and my French is good enough to do the occasional translation – I have even let myself believe that my accent is charming and *très* Jane Birkin. But as soon as I reach the Gare de Montparnasse, I feel like a badly dressed nerd who doesn't speak a word of French.

Now I'm worried Daisy is going to be transformed into a hyper-sophisticated *Parisienne* who will cast withering glances at my footwear. I do make a bit more effort with my grooming these days, but I don't go over the top and Paris seems to me to be the sort of place where you are expected to brush your hair every day and wear matching socks.

But after all Daisy's still at school, doing the last year of her baccalaureate, how glamorous can it be?

I put her on the train with heavy heart – and heavy luggage.

'What the hell is in here?

'Make up and philosophy books.'

I ring up a couple of weeks later to see how Daisy's doing.

The school is a big success, she turns out to be a natural-born philosopher, and philosophy is a hugely important part of the bac in the last year. Even her dress sense is appreciated. One day she goes in wearing a leopard skin coat.

'*J'adore*,' says the headmistress, 'You're like the school cat!'

Leopard skin is not so misunderstood as it was in my day.

'What did you do at the weekend, sweetie? I hope you didn't miss me too much.'

'Not really. It was the *Nuit Blanche* when everything stays open all night, not just the bars and cancan clubs, but museums, art galleries and bookshops. We went to St-Germain-des-Prés and drank champagne and then I went to a party with Henri Cartier-Bresson's granddaughter. How about you?'

Damn, how could I compete with that?

'I went for a surf.' I knew that wasn't going to impress her so I quickly added, 'Then I went over to Taryn and Steve's and drank rosé in the Jacuzzi.' That sounded suitably Malibu Beach – thank God for glamorous friends.

'Oh! Mum, can you send me some money for a sports kit?'

'Didn't I do that already?'

'Yes, but I bought some hats at Galeries Lafayette, remember?'

'Well, can't I send you my trainers? I've got no money.' Oh no, classic mummy-turning-into-martyr line.

'Well, the trouble is, I can't wear nylon trainers, they have to be leather.' Here's my point: Paris is so chic that you can't even wear nylon trainers for a sport's lesson. God knows what happens if you wear them in the street. You probably get arrested by the style police and given a one-way ticket to Clermont-Ferrand.

'So, if you haven't got a sports kit, what have you been wearing for badminton?'

'My Mickey Mouse pyjamas.'

I heaved a sigh of relief. She still needed me.

100 PER CENT MAMAS

Johanna, the founder of the Mamas, is a mama now, so her daughter Lina starts surfing young of course – very young. Even I'm surprised when Christophe brings their adorable blonde five-month-old baby to the beach in a lifejacket. He paddles out with her and Johanna on a tandem board, takes a wave and sweeps Lina up onto his shoulders. It's only a knee-high wave, but I have to tell several alarmed tourists on the beach that he's not crazy – he's a surfer.

We're pretty sure she's just broken the record for the youngest person ever to take a wave at Olatua. They've brought a bottle of champagne down to the beach to celebrate the unusual christening ceremony of the latest addition to the Reinhardt surf dynasty. I'm not sure if Lina knows what's going on as we toast her historic moment, but she seems to be enjoying the attention.

She's also one more woman in the water. Since we started there are a lot more women, many from the other women's surf clubs and there are younger girls coming out as well.

Of the original Mamas about half have kept going, some have moved away, one is about to have another baby, some just don't take to it. In the end you have to be a bit obsessive to learn to surf and to get through the first couple of years when you spend a lot more time wiping out than riding on the crest of the ocean wave.

Other women join, and a lot of them are French, which is exciting.

But not all women have the secret desire to become a surf bum as I found out when I asked a friend's girlfriend if she might be interested at a party.

She was a bit drunk and I thought for a moment she was going to hit me.

'No! I fucking *hate* surfing. Things aren't going well between us. Do you want to know why? I'm going out with a 45-year-old man who's an eternal teenager all because of surfing. Don't talk to me about it.'

It didn't seem a good moment to suggest that if she discovered her own inner teenage surf bum they might get on better.

It's not unusual when you hear that a couple have split up for the first question to be: 'Was it the surf or an affair?'

And not all men want their partners to surf, so we move the weekly rendezvous to Fridays because the novelty of being a Surf Widow wears off after a bit. I think a lot of the husbands and boyfriends thought: How sweet, the girls are trying to learn to surf. They did not expect to find themselves married to an obsessive surf maniac.

They're also not so charmed when they come home after a hard day at the office and ask, 'What's for dinner?'

Only to be told, 'I'm all surfed out, how about a bowl of corn flakes?'

Before the Mamas started, the percentage of women in the water in Guéthary was about one per cent – consisting of Isabelle, Christophe's cousin and his daughter Valentine, now an artist in Paris. Now it's perhaps 10 per cent. On a good day.

So it's quite an exciting event when we reverse the statistics – although we have to take extreme measures.

I go round to Taryn's house. She's working on a sculpture of a Japanese woman's head and listening to a Japanese language tape.

'I'm going back to Japan; I'm so damn excited! And we're going to surf there.'

'I'm so damn jealous!'

'Yeah, but, I don't know what's wrong with me; I've got no motivation to surf today at all! I don't know why... ' Taryn says, sounding disappointed in herself.

I think for a moment that she's joking, but apparently not.

'Maybe it's something to do with *that!*'

I point to the window, outside it's like a winter wonderland, a thick layer of snow on the beach, which is weird because it's spring and we hardly ever get snow even in midwinter.

'I know, but wouldn't it be cool to be out there all alone with the snow falling all around.'

'Maybe if you were a penguin or a walrus, Taryn!' I laugh.

Two days later the snow has melted and I'm walking along the beach thinking, yes, maybe today. Until I turn the corner and the north wind cuts through my fleece jacket and I think, maybe not. But I feel quite brave just for having had the thought and give myself a pat on the back.

Then I see a woman about my age jogging along the beach. She stops by a rock, strips off and runs into the sea naked. I'm as impressed as the Russian lorry drivers walking in the other direction. I feel like she's thrown down the gauntlet, along with her Nikes, tracksuit trousers and sweatshirt.

I get home and phone Taryn. 'We have to surf, I saw a naked woman swimming on the beach.'

'What? Why? Are there waves?'

'Er, not many. But who needs waves when you've got sunshine, an empty ocean and a bracing onshore gale blowing?'

We meet Johanna at the beach checking the swell, and she doesn't need too much persuading to come in with us. 'It's not snowing anymore and there's no one else out.'

Johanna's spent most of the winter in Verbier where she's a ski instructor. There hasn't been much powder snow this year, so she wasn't very amused to get home last week and find herself surrounded by the stuff and nothing to do with it but make snowmen.

She leaves Lina with Christophe and the three of us paddle out together.

The ice-cream head hits before we even get wet, but there are a few waves. We stay out for a while, so happy to have it to ourselves. We're on the big wave that breaks way out, and we wonder whether there has *ever* been an all-women surf session out here. It feels like a historic moment and well worth the frostbite risk. Eventually a male surfer joins us.

'Wow!' he says, 'I don't believe it, one hundred per cent *nanas.*' *Nanas* being French slang for 'hot chicks'.

'No,' we correct him, 'one hundred per cent Mamas.'

THE SUN ALSO RISES

Summer comes bringing fiesta season and the mood in Olatua changes dramatically day by day according to the direction of the wind and height of swell, as it also changes from season to season. In winter Olatua can seem like a ghost town, autumn is surf season when it fills up with surf pros and VW vans full of German new-agers living the dream. July and August is party season. The village is packed, the bars are packed, the wave is packed. Apart from the usual crowd you have to negotiate swimmers, divers harpooning octopus, rubber dinghies and jet skis.

It's fiesta every night in the village square: balls where couples dance to old-fashioned accordion music, Basque heavy-metal gigs. There's a by-law prohibiting all manual labour for the month of August to keep the noise down, but you can't stop the music: bongo drums, Johnny Hallyday tributes and reggae bands, and if you're lucky you might even hear my very own Daisy Tallulah singing '*La Vie En Rose*' or 'Gimme A Pigfoot' in one of the bars when she returns from Paris for the summer.

By 1 August it's all too much and the Beautiful People leave town or lock themselves in the studio until the plukes go home.

(Plukes is a term of abuse for inhabitants of the French desert I learned from my children. *Parisien* can also be used as an insult on the Côte Basque; but as far as tourists go, if there's anything worse than being *Parisien* it's not being *Parisien*.)

I love party season, I wouldn't miss the Mamas barbecue or the annual Olatua Sardine Night for anything, but I'm not so good on the huge fiestas like the Fêtes de Bayonne and San Fermín in Pamplona, which over a million people attend every year.

Pamplona is the setting for Ernest Hemingway's classic *Fiesta* (also published as *The Sun Also Rises*) and every year people fly from all over the world to relive the fire and passion of his masterpiece by getting hopelessly drunk, falling hopelessly in love and watching bulls being killed by matadors and tourists being trampled by bulls.

I always feel a bit of a wimp not taking the 90-minute trip up the road to check it out. But I hate crowds, I don't do well in the heat and there's no reason to think being chased by a herd of bulls would improve the situation.

Nor am I at all sure what I think of the ritual slaughter of bulls by men in tights. People tell me you have to understand the *corrida* before you can condemn it. But I suspect if I had got to Pamplona I'd have joined the body-painted animal-rights protesters who've been holding nude press conferences and parading the streets in fake blood and G-strings.

People also tell me you have to go with the right people if you want to enjoy it, and you certainly don't want to go alone. Or with your kids, I imagine.

Well, I did attempt to go that summer. I was in the bar with a friend I'd met in the water, who looked as if he came from a long line of toreadors. I think the hot south wind and the cold rosé were affecting my brain – I was imagining a torrid and intense brief encounter, made all the more torrid and intense by the imminent danger of being gored by a rogue bull or dying of sangria poisoning. But instead of offering to whisk me off into the sierra, he got out his iPhone and started showing me photos of his baby son. Either he hadn't read the book or he was worried that I'd take off with a macho young matador and break his heart. I reluctantly dropped my Hemingwayesque *femme fatale* persona and reverted to agony aunt.

'Do you think I should try again with the mother of my child?' he wanted to know.

'I suppose you might as well, if you're not taking me to San Fermín,' I said and went off in a sulk wondering if there were any real men left. I wasn't seriously expecting an attack of *l'amour fou*. We always flirted with each other a bit, but then again everyone flirts with everyone in France, people even flirt with my dog. My moodiness was sparked off more by the thought that life was getting too sensible. Hemingway would never have written a novel involving iPhones and responsible parenting.

Someone had stuck a leaflet under the windscreen of my car advertising the Toro Piscine, an hour of 'laughing games with cows' on a beach in the caravan park zone down the road. Probably the 'funniest laughing cows show in the world', it promised. Hopefully the *only* laughing cows show in the world, I thought, looking at the photos of tourists in bad shorts being tossed into paddling pools by veal calves. It was like a *Carry On* version of *Fiesta*.

By the time I got to my favourite bar, Heteroclito, I felt as if the spirit of Don Ernesto might have abandoned us altogether. I'd gone to meet Phil and Trudi who were with some young Australian cousins on their way to Pamplona, and Jeff Hakman.

Jeff was world champion during the early days of professional surfing, winning every contest on the global tour. He lived the dream and then survived the nightmare when the decade-long party of the 1960s spiralled into the decade-long hangover of the 1970s. Now he's between a boat trip in the Indian Ocean and a trip to Mexico, and sitting next to me looking like an ad for the rejuvenating powers of saltwater and the rock 'n' roll lifestyle.

'What do you think about bullfighting?' I asked him, sticking with the theme and hoping he wasn't going to tell me he preferred the laughing cows show or get out some baby pictures.

'Oh, I tried it once, but I wouldn't do it again.'

'You went to a bullfight once?'

'No, I was in one.'

He told me he was in Peru during the early wilder days of the world tour. Jeff had won the championship and the after party was epic. It was still in mid-swing in the middle of the night when his hosts shoved him in a car with a bottle of wine, and told him it was time to 'fight the bull', which he assumed was some kind of Peruvian joke.

The next thing he knew he was in the bullring in his board shorts and a cape in front of a cheering crowd, wishing he'd listened more closely to bullfighting lessons at school...

'What did you do?'

'Not much, I waited until the bull turned away and got out of there as quick as I could!' he laughed.

He's a surf legend, not a bullfighter – he doesn't need the ears and the tail to impress me.

SURF ADDICT

My name is Wilma… and I'm a surf addict.

With Daisy in Paris and my disastrous attempts at dating on hold, I spend a lot of time in the water.

The Mamas Surf Club continues meeting and as time goes by we improve, sometimes even looking for bigger rather than smaller waves, *expecting* to stand up rather than counting it as a minor miracle. It no longer counts as a 'good session' if I come out of the water with no visible bruising or dings on my board.

Now we are really surfing, doing complicated manoeuvres like turning, which is a relief during Mamas sessions as we crash into each other a lot less frequently.

I wonder sometimes what kept us going back when the odds seemed against us ever getting beyond the white wash.

'I think it was the social side,' Taryn says. 'Some days I couldn't wait to get out of the water and talk to the girls.'

It's true that there's nothing like living through a seemingly life threatening adrenalin charged experience for a bit of bonding. I can laugh about it now, but we were genuinely terrified at first, having to literally hold hands out at sea and calm each other down with yogic breathing and reassurances that we'd look after each other's kids if we didn't make it back to the beach.

One day I'm walking along the beach in summer and I see a lot of surf schools and beginners surfing in the foam a few metres from the sand. I watch one woman get to her feet, scream and punch her hands in the air before doing a face plant in the sand.

Her friends in the water whoop and cheer.

'Sweet,' I think, laughing to myself.

Then I realise that it's happening all the way down the beach, people getting to their feet for a split second, collapsing into the water and then jumping up, cheering in excitement, carried away in ecstasy like Baptist holy rollers.

I remember the feeling. It's why we ignored the bruises, the wipeouts, the cold water and the total humiliation, for those few seconds of excitement and the tantalising idea that it might eventually lead to riding a wave.

And it did.

After one of the sessions I remind Christophe of the days when he used to have to drag me back out by my leash, kicking and screaming in 50-centimetre waves.

'Did you ever really think you'd be able to teach me to surf?' I was touched by his belief that I might one day be able to paddle out back and take a wave by myself, standing up even, but I thought he'd seriously overestimated my potential.

'I can teach anyone to stand up, that's the easy part. But what really impressed me about the Mamas was the determination.

I wasn't sure that you would keep going, but *you* seem so motivated. More than that… what's the word?'

'Obsessed?' I suggest.

'No,' Johanna corrects me, 'the word is *addicted*!'

'That's it Wilma, surfing is my addiction and I love getting other people hooked.' Christophe laughs.

Johanna's right. I've been ignoring the signs for a while, but the other day I had to admit I had a problem.

Quite often I find myself surfing without even knowing why I'm doing it – because it's there, I suppose. I automatically head out into the water whenever I get a bit of free time. Of course I never really have totally free time, but sometimes I decide that my painting looks nicer a bit unfinished, I can't pay the bills anyway so there's not much point opening them, the kids can have microwave popcorn for supper. Then I slip into a trance-like state as I pack my wetsuit bag, strap my board on the roof of the car and drive to the beach. I might be halfway out to the wave before I come to my senses, probably as a result of a few tons of ice-cold water landing on my head, and wonder why the hell I'm here surfing. Surely I could have found something easier, more relaxing, more sane to do for fun?

One day when I'm complaining about chronic exhaustion, Daisy asks me: 'Have you ever thought that you might be tired because every time you get a chance to relax you go surfing and get even more tired?'

This thought wouldn't cross my mind on a nice summer day with metre-high waves and an offshore wind. It only occurs to me when it's too big, too cold, too windy, too polluted or all of the above. That's when I think I should have looked a bit harder from the beach as I might have realised that those aren't really small people surfing on tiny boards, they're really big waves. I might have noticed the sign warning that the water is infested with jellyfish or that a thunderstorm is moving in from Spain. But I get overexcited and paddle out without looking around. Once I get a wave it all makes sense and I know I've done the right thing, but the other morning it was hard to shake the feeling that I'd gone a bit mad. Or was suffering from addictive behaviour.

When I woke up I didn't feel great. I was hoping I was still asleep and having a nightmare about the worst hangover in the world. It was the morning after the Beaujolais party in the village. Nobody drinks Beaujolais Nouveau except on the night the new vintage is released, for the simple reason that it's not very nice. That's why we feel obliged to drink a whole year's ration in one go in order to keep the grape pickers and vineyard owners in business. It takes about 364 days to get over the hangover, just in time for the next vintage.

I was finding it hard to accept that a person of my age and maturity could be stupid enough to make themselves feel so ill, so I was lying in bed looking for someone or something else to blame: I'd been drugged, excessive sulphates in the wine, allergic reaction to the colouring in that one slice of chorizo (the *only* food I'd eaten *all* evening), the fault of the twenty-something-year-old longboarder who had insisted on buying me one for the road.

Then the phone rang. It was Johanna telling me that she and the Mamas were heading down to the bay of St-Jean-de-Luz for a surf. I could hear the waves from my window, a kilometre inland, which should have been a warning. But I was remembering the theory that fresh air and saltwater are a perfect hangover cure. I was too hungover to paint. I was too hungover to drink a cup of tea, which (if I wasn't suffering from surf addiction) might also have told me something.

For the second time in 12 hours I gave in to temptation. (Not the third, just for the record.)

I couldn't feel any worse I thought optimistically as I went in to the garden to get my wetsuit, which was damp and slightly rigid with frost.

It's a mistake to think you can't feel any worse. Maybe I didn't feel any worse, maybe I felt exactly the same, but instead of being in bed I was a kilometre out to sea with 2-metre waves breaking all around me and a gale-force wind blowing me towards the sea wall. It hit me about half an hour too late that when the world is spinning around, your head is about to explode and drinking water makes you queasy, it might be a good idea to be lying under your duvet with an Alka-Seltzer and a phone beside you with SOS Médecins on speed dial. It might not be quite such a good idea to be sitting in the ocean like a shipwreck survivor on a piece of fibreglass that is attached to your leg by a strip of Velcro. I've never thought Velcro was much good as a fastening for a gym slip or a hospital gown, and now I was relying on it to get me home in one piece.

I was no longer able to justify my behaviour by thinking: *I'm a surfer*. I started thinking: *I'm completely mad*.

It was a very dramatic and beautiful scene. One side of the sky was bright blue, the other piled up with black storm clouds. The candy-pink casinos and hotels of St-Jean-de-Luz curved round the bay with snow-covered mountains behind. The waves rolled in from the Bay of Biscay, crashing over the sea wall and sending plumes of spray in to the sky as they made their way towards me. I kept paddling further and further from the impact zone until I could no longer hear my cheerful healthy surf buddies laughing and yelling, 'Paddle harder, Wilma.' I'd given up on the idea of catching a wave long ago, I was just hoping to get through the session without embarrassing myself by throwing up in the water or dying.

The icing on the cake was the guilt trip I was putting myself through wondering what would happen if I did die of alcohol poisoning out here. I would leave three motherless children to fend for themselves in a harsh world just because I got carried away chatting up a Californian longboarder half my age. I could see the headlines in the local paper: 'Englishwoman Wins Posthumous Bad Parenting Award', 'Selfish Cougar Lost At Sea'.

The swell was building and I couldn't find a calm spot. When I was almost hit by a dead cormorant I decided it was time to call it a day and I paddled in to the beach. It's a bit of a cop out to go in without even trying to take a wave, but sometimes it's better to cop out than cop it. I made it back to dry land, but I was so cold and weak I couldn't get out of my wetsuit and had to ask the Mamas for help, which was pathetic and humiliating. I don't think I've ever appreciated a bubble bath so much in all my life.

The surf cure worked, even if it was a bit extreme, because a few hours later I felt energetic enough to go to a Zumba class. And, of course, the next time I had a hangover I did exactly the same thing and I was fine, so now I'm thinking that perhaps it *was* the additives in the wine after all.

Another case of surfaholic behaviour soon follows. I've got used to surfing alone, although ideally I like to be there with a couple of Mamas so we can chat between sets, admire each other's waves and share make-up tips. Sometimes it is hard to find the right moment to get in the water between school runs and work and onshore winds, and if you try to fit in with your friends' school runs, you're going to miss waves. Sometimes you have to be tough and say to other Mamas: 'I'm sorry you've got a teachers' meeting, I'll see you out there.'

Paddling out alone is not the same as surfing alone. I have paddled out alone after counting 120 people in the water.

It can be quite eerie to be by yourself out there. You start wondering *why* you're alone. Maybe the waves are too small or it's too windy, which suits me fine. Maybe you're just lucky or maybe there's a plague of jellyfish or a freak migration of sharks – or maybe you are about to be struck by lightning.

Things didn't look great when I got to the beach: the water was dark, the sky was darker, the waves were blown out, but I was feeling stressed about my next show in Biarritz and it *was* Sunday after all. I knew I'd made the right decision as soon as the first wave broke over my head, emptying my mind of anything less important than how to avoid the big set crashing over me and washing me up on the reef.

There were a few other surfers out, all dreaming of the Perfect Wave though we all knew deep down that we weren't going to find it today.

'Only the faithful,' someone laughed when I joined them. Well, that's what I thought the word *fidèle* meant, but in this case it might have had a slightly different meaning, like 'totally deranged'.

It was like an offshore meeting of Surfaholics Anonymous. We all had excuses for being out there.

'It's not snowing anymore.'

'My mother-in-law has come to stay, I had to get out of the house.'

'My wife kicked me out, I'm living in the van.'

'I'm training for a contest in Tahiti.'

'My exhibition doesn't start until next week! Anyone want to come?'

There was a long wait between sets and we spent a while admiring the spectacular view of a thunderstorm over San Sebastián, forks of lightning turning the sky phosphorescent green like a distant firework display, and caught some less than spectacular waves.

The south wind had picked up and, like the mistral in the Mediterranean, it can be held responsible for eccentric behaviour, crimes of passion and bad surfing. The thunder moved closer.

'Time to go I think,' said someone and the rest of the line-up, men with quicker reactions than me, turned in unison and caught a wave, like a group of Waikiki beach boys.

Ukulele music mingled with the seagulls' screams, and they were halfway to warm cars and cold beers by the time I realised I was alone.

Be careful what you wish for – the cornerstone of fortune cookie philosophy came back to me. I had often wished I had the wave to myself, now I was wishing there was someone out here with me so I didn't feel so much like a lightning conductor – a tall surfer perhaps or, even better, a stand-up paddle boarder to take the hit for me.

Although it would be a dramatic exit from the world I'm not ready to be struck by lightning. I've got paintings to finish, places to go and three children expecting me to provide them with unconditional love, spiritual guidance and frozen pizza. And it would be a shame to go before I learned to hang five.

There are times when you want a wave and times when you need a wave – like right now. When I see a big frothy white horse moving towards me I paddle in a frenzy against the gale force wind, take off and stay superglued to the board from sheer determination, even though there's so much spray in my eyes I can't see where I'm going.

The wave takes me over the reef and into the flat calm of the lagoon. I'm about to lie down and paddle when I realise that the wind is so strong, my body is acting as a sail and I keep being pushed across the dark flat water with lightning flashing around me. As I reach the beach the sun breaks through, the scene is illuminated by orange evening sunlight and the raindrops turn into huge hailstones.

It's like a scene from a Victorian religious painting and I feel I should step onto the beach with some divine revelation for my disciples. But the beach is empty apart from a dead cuttlefish and my very wet and patient dog.

Apart from being overwhelmed by the beauty of the moment I'm hoping to God there's hot water in the tank, and thinking it would be cool if I had a G&T in my hand to catch the heaven-sent ice cubes.

I chuck a plastic bag onto the seat of the car – a futile gesture as the roof is leaking and there's a pool of water on the floor – and drive up to the Addams Family Mansion, which is looking more atmospheric than ever with the backdrop of the electric storm. I'm half expecting Boris Karloff to open the door with a glass of blood on a silver platter.

AN EVENING AT THE PALAIS THERMAL

Things go into a meltdown around Halloween starting with a disastrous show at Palais Thermal, an elegant old spa in the centre of Biarritz. I should never have been tempted, but when a plastic surgeon asks me to show in his new gallery, Salle d'Attente, I didn't realise that it was literally in his waiting room. It *was* a beautiful space, the Art Deco grandeur and plush red carpets seemed like a good setting for my *Goddesses* series. If I'd thought about it rationally I'd have realised that I don't have any clients in Biarritz, so it's not a great idea. The surgeon had a very persuasive manner and I was a bit drunk, so under the circumstances I guess it was lucky he wasn't trying to sell me a facelift or a boob job.

I've been working all year on a collection of large scale paintings of goddesses, starting with Venus and the Three Graces, but soon Eve slips in, then a version of Degas' *Absinthe Drinker* and a couple of self-portraits. I call the show 'Venus, Eve and the Absinthe Drinker' and subtitle it 'Goddesses and

Fallen Women from the Garden of Eden to Montmartre', which all sounds rather grand and doesn't put the self-portraits specifically in either camp.

I've got obsessed with these paintings, which are getting bigger and bigger and therefore more and more expensive to make.

'Why would you buy gold leaf instead of giving me pocket money?' Nat asks. It's a tough question.

Because I'm an artist. Because I believe that one day my paintings will be worth millions and I will be able to buy a mansion on the Grande Plage, bathe in champagne and double your pocket money. But for now you have to eat pasta pesto again because I've spent all the money on gold leaf and cadmium pigments.

Being an artist is like being a gambler, you believe you're on the verge of a big win, and all artists think they've got four aces in their hand or they would have given up long ago. Perversely, when an artist is on a losing streak they tend to raise the stakes: make the paintings bigger and use more expensive paint to make something so beautiful and so big that no one can ignore it or resist buying it. Covered in gold leaf and cadmium. Double or quits.

This explanation does very little to placate Nat who is convinced that *Grand Theft Auto* would be a much better use of money.

While I finish the work for the show, I imagine how cool it would be if his clients fell under the spell of my paintings, and asked the surgeon to make them look like the women on my canvases. I would see living versions of my paintings walking along the Grande Plage and I would feel like Dr Frankenstein or God. The thought cheers me up.

The building has a high-ceilinged baroque-style grandeur that suits my work perfectly and there is a neat row of silicon breast implants, which look rather like jellyfish, on a shelf under my painting of Venus. I like the surreal touch, but I wonder if it's a bit of competition. Can you trust people to make the right choice between a new painting and a new cleavage? I also feel like my painting is being used as encouragement to aspire to a perfect goddess-like body.

I've planned everything to the last detail: the organic Bordeaux, the bowl of exotic fruits, the platter of exquisite miniature pastries. The only thing I hadn't planned was the apocalyptic storm that came sweeping in off the Bay of Biscay. We were in the middle of 62 days of torrential rain and thought we'd seen everything the weather could throw at us, but the combination of the highest tide of the year, a big swell and more rain in one day than usually falls in a month had flooded Bayonne. All the roads were closed, the trains were cancelled and the motorway was blocked by a massive pile-up.

It wasn't just wet on the outside; my house and my car were flooded. It was surprising that the accelerator worked as it was under water. I arrived at the gallery very wet and wondering why I'd bothered to buy new espadrilles instead of picking up some old rope off the beach and gluing it to my feet.

I could have coped with the flooding, a few roadblocks, south-west France grinding to a total standstill except I had lost Daisy somewhere in the French desert between Dax and here on a train that had been stopped by the extreme weather conditions. Daisy was coming back for the weekend, either homesick or exhausted by her busy social life. I was in a puritanical phase during which I believed that mobile phones are not only a waste of money but are electronic tracking devices, an abuse of personal freedom. It felt like the final straw when the home phone line blew down as I was leaving.

I spent the entire evening completely stressed, imagining Daisy swimming through floodwater or stuck overnight in some redneck railway station without money, phone and no way of contacting MUMMY. I was fully expecting to have to take the flooded car through the floodwaters to find her.

'Can you explain your painting process?' asked a private view guest.

'Not right now. Do you know anything about this freak wave that has just flooded Bayonne railway station?'

I finally manage to get through to a friend of Daisy's and find out that my daughter was not stuck in a railway station waiting room or a derailed TGV. In fact, keeping a clear head in an emergency, she'd had the presence of mind to get out of the train at Bordeaux, ring some friends and go to a party in the ultra-chic beach resort of Cap Ferret where she was drinking champagne and eating oysters.

Now that I didn't have to worry about Daisy, I could worry about the show and notice the spectacular absence of red dots. I don't think anyone even bought a catalogue.

My goddesses stared down at me from behind the breast implants and my absinthe drinker ordered another round.

HAPPY HALLOWEEN

Not long after the show I get a letter saying the house has been deemed unfit to live in because of the electricity. We knew that all along but we loved the Addams Family Mansion all the same, so this is a bit of a blow, especially as it's notoriously difficult to rent places locally. We have to move out by 1 January, which doesn't give me long to find a new place for me, my kids, my growing menagerie, my surfboard, my easels, and all those goddesses and fallen women will need a home as they haven't sold.

Then my car breaks down twice in one week – the first time was acceptable, just a flat tyre.

I'm not a great mechanic, but changing a tyre is one thing I know how to do. You just undo your top button, put on a bit of lip gloss and stand in the middle of the road. It works every time. After ten minutes I have four charming Frenchmen gathered round the car. I don't feel bad about this; I think they quite like it. After all the bullshit we women have given men – burning our bras, not shaving our armpits, asking for equal pay and the vote – it's nice for them to see a return to good old-fashioned values. It validates their position in society.

Except that in this case it doesn't work. They can't get the damn wheel off as it's rusted onto the thingy. One by one they drift off, feeling useless and confused again in this brave new world of designer sperm banks, hairy armpits and rusty wheel thingies.

Two days later a real man with a pick-up truck and a crowbar comes and changes the tyre, but the spare is flat so he tows the car to the garage.

The mechanic tells me it's a heap of junk and that it's not worth the expense of buying two new tyres. He'll order just one tyre and suggests I buy the hideous white Renault that is rusting on his forecourt. I refuse, insulted. My car may be old – it's a 1984 Mercedes – but it has class and style and it can accommodate a 10-foot longboard. In certain lights it could be seen as a collector's item.

It's a very cool car, but it would be even cooler if it moved. I could forgive it for one breakdown this week, but the second one is too much. I try to hold it together and to keep a calm, controlled, grown-up facade in place for the sake of my youngest daughter. But the car becomes a symbol for everything that's wrong in my life and I let the mask slip.

'You goddamn stupid fucking heap of shit.' I kick it a few times. 'Alice, I am nearly fifty fucking years old, can you explain to me why I can't have a car that starts? Can you? I can. It's because I'm a stupid goddamn fucking ARTIST!' I drift into a morose monologue. 'I should have been an accountant, we have nowhere to live, I want to go for a fucking surf, I who have nothing.'

'Never mind, you've got me, Mummy,' Alice says cheerfully. 'I'll give you a massage.'

Before I can calm down, my psychotically needy sheepdog joins in. She throws herself through the air like a poltergeist from a horror movie, all hair and claws and fangs, and hits me in the chest. 'Never mind, you've got ME, Mummy!'

'Get off me, you stupid animal, I don't want you. I want a car.'

Then I feel guilty. I go inside and give Bibi a tin of wet dog food as a treat and I ring the garage.

'Oh no, not again. Why don't you buy a new Mercedes?'

Because I spent all my money on gold leaf.

I ring Taryn.

'What am I going to do? My life is falling apart.'

'Throw a party,' she says without hesitation.

'I don't feel like it, and anyway I spent all my money on gold leaf.'

'You have to – it's Halloween. People are buying their costumes already.'

Throwing a party, like going for a surf, is something I'm easily persuaded to do. It is clear to everyone, especially me, that my house is the best place to celebrate the night of the living dead.

The Mamas have rallied round with onshore solidarity. They've all said they'll bring food and help me get the house ready in view of my recent meltdown.

But there's a slight change of plan when the swell comes up.

Taryn calls to say she'll pick me up in ten minutes.

I look around the house – it doesn't really have to be cleaned up for Halloween. I can leave the cobwebs and add another layer. I chuck a few plastic spiders around and tell the children to do their worst.

'But what about the food? Should I be cooking?' I ask Taryn.

'Don't worry, I went to the market and ordered a platter of oysters for you. They're delivering them at dusk and I'm bringing a box of Steve's rosé.'

The oyster stall in Biarritz market has the best oysters in town and the best looking fishmongers in town deliver them ready shucked on a platter.

'Great, thanks. I'll pick up some frozen canapés from Picard on the way home.'

When I get back from the beach there's no time to spare.

'What about your costume?' asks a group of charming ghouls.

I'd forgotten about my costume. Give me a minute.

I throw on a black Lycra dress, and go in to the garden to pick the dead flowers and some ivy and laurel, which I wrap around my head: a laurel wreath for services to surf.

'There, do I look OK?'

My son is doubtful. 'I don't know Mum, you don't look much like a witch, more like a goddess.'

We all laugh because Nat's not big for paying lavish compliments.

'I didn't *mean* it like that,' he protests, but I decide not to change.

Taryn goes home and varnishes her nails black, Florence puts on more black eyeliner than usual and Jo gets a pair of flashing red horns from the dressing-up box.

The four of us are leaning on the bar when a friend arrives with blood dripping down her forehead and an axe in her skull. '*Oh là là*,' she says in mock disgust, 'look at the Mamas Surf Club. You're meant to be *witches* girls, not beach babes.'

It does seem a shame to invite the Beautiful People round and greet them looking like the Bride of Frankenstein, even if they do. I think the beach babe/goddess look was a necessary ego boost after all the yoga and wipeouts.

Everyone comes, I think. I never know who all the guests are and there are always a few who arrive and leave without my ever knowing who they are.

Bibi becomes hysterical and barks until she is hoarse. She takes her guard dog duties very seriously and although she loves me she doesn't think I'm too bright. Seeing me welcoming werewolves and vampires, armed with bloody axes and scythes, into the house proves the point and she goes into a meltdown.

To add insult to injury, I'm offering the guests food Bibi would have happily eaten herself: the huge platter of oysters, the Picard selection of ready-to-bake canapés and snail vol-au-vents – chic yet vaguely spooky.

A surfer I met in the water earlier comes to the party and buys a big painting, *Surf Mama*. Like all artists I get emotionally attached to my paintings and I like to see them go to good homes, so I'm glad that she'll be hanging in a house on the cliff with a view of the wave at Olatua!

His daughters have brought confetti, so we celebrate by drinking champagne and letting the kids throw confetti all around the house, along with sweets, plastic spiders and tubs of glitter and sequins. The picture sale takes on the feeling of an Indian festival.

This is the way to sell paintings, I think, and a refreshing take on networking. Cut out the gallery system, just paddle out and find prospective buyers in the water.

FREAKING ENORMOUS

I wake up to a surreal scene the next morning: confetti, sugar snakes and cobwebs carpet the stairs; empty wine bottles and bowls of fake eyeballs, fangs and witches fingers litter the kitchen; and Bibi is chewing a plastic snake. The entire house is carpeted with coloured confetti that looks so pretty I leave it for a few days. The kitchen isn't so pretty and I don't even want to look in the basement.

I still have no gallery, no money and no millionaire. My car's broken down and I have notice to quit my house. But it doesn't really matter because I've got a surfboard, a wetsuit and a friend with a roof rack.

I call Taryn.

'Are we surfing again today?'

'I'm looking out of my window. Hang on, is that a seagull out there? No, it's a surfer. Holy shit, Wilma, it's fucking enormous!'

'I know, I know. I thought we could go down to Hendaye where it might be slightly less fucking enormous.'

'OK, if you're sure.'

269

'I've never been more sure of anything in my life.'

I phone Jo. Jo is in worse meltdown than I am. She's splitting up with her husband and shortly going back to England for a while.

'I'll meet you down there,' she says.

Half an hour later Jo, Taryn and I are getting changed on the promenade, yet again providing free entertainment for the Spanish couples walking by in their hats and gloves. This time there are a couple of slightly drunk German tourists too, and they're taking photos of us. The Bay of Biscay is definitely in sea shanty mode today.

I squeeze myself into a wet neoprene body stocking, fight my way through a pounding shore break and paddle into the middle of a group of tough-looking Basque men. I've heard that in some parts of the world, Malibu Beach and other places, there are a lot of women in the water, but in Hendaye on a wild winter afternoon with a big swell running, the line-up is 100 per cent men and the men are 100 per cent macho. These men don't think that gender differences are the result of social conditioning, they're not even contemplating getting in touch with their feminine side and they do not think it's all right to wear a bit of eyeliner if you feel like it. But they do have nice shoulders.

I don't usually wear make up, but I always put on a dab of lip gloss and some waterproof mascara before I get in the water. (And if it's at all possible, I wear a bikini because you do get more waves that way. But not in winter.) If you think you only have to watch your look on land round here, forget it. You never know who you're going to meet in the line-up.

Like most things in life, you can see the positive or the negative side. Oh no, I'm the only woman out here. Oh yes, I'm the only woman out here.

The age of chivalry is not dead on the coast, and as a woman you're more likely to get chatted up than beaten up if you drop in on someone's wave. As long as you only do it once. Out here today there are a group of young surfers with tattoos, dreadlocks and pierced faces, a bit like a group of wet Hell's Angels.

I smile and say, 'Bonjour.' Can't go wrong with that, can you?

'Hola.' OK, yes you can. They look worried. Perhaps they're thinking: Oh no, are we going to have to rescue this one and if it comes to it, is she worth it? Or they might be wondering: What's going on? This is my rebellion – youth against the establishment – what's this mama lady doing out here?

I paddle out further than the rest of the line-up because I've got a big board. I paddle so far out that Taryn and Jo start wondering if I've lost my nerve.

I see a big set coming, the sort of waves that would usually have me paddling for the horizon like a wind-up bath toy. But today I think: Oh what the hell, you're only young twice, go for it!

There's not much point describing a wave. Being a surfer is like being a born-again Christian, you can only talk about it to the saved. If you surf you'll know exactly how it feels to catch the biggest wave of your life; if you don't, you've probably glazed over.

This doesn't feel like the biggest wave I've ever caught, it feels like the biggest wave anyone has ever caught in the history of the world. When I come in past the tough Basque guys, they whistle and cheer. Which is cool because not long ago they were looking at me nervously, wondering which way I was going to fall.

We all know it's about that pure moment between you and the ocean; we're all soul surfers at heart. But we're all big kids too.

I paddle back out to the girls. 'Did you see my wave? It seemed kind of big,' I say as casually as I can. I'm sick of being told my big waves were 20 centimetres high.

'Big? It was fucking enormous.'

This is it. I'm a gnarly surf dude at last.

'Has my mascara run?'

On the way home in the car Taryn and I are comparing our boards.

'So you think three fins would be better for me than a single fin, although perhaps you need that big fin to stop you spinning out?'

'Yes, and mine's got a narrow tail and a lot of rocker so… '

I hear myself, and start laughing.

'Does it ever freak you out when you hear yourself talking like that?'

Taryn laughs, and then goes quiet.

'No. You know what really freaked me out, Wilma? The other day I heard myself discussing recipes for carrot cake. *That* freaked me out.'

There's a silence.

'God, that's horrible. Shall we stop for a beer?'

'Don't worry, I put some in the fridge and turned on the Jacuzzi before I left.'

'Awesome.'

Part Five

BASKETBALL MUM
AND THE EMPTY NEST

A couple of years later...

We've moved out of the Addams Family Mansion, Halloween will never be the same again, but the role of Morticia was taking over my persona.

The new place is a two and a half bedroom semi in the centre of the village. It's not as atmospheric, although I do still hear screech owls and bats at night; maybe they followed me here. The scariest thing is the sound of the dentist's drill coming through the wall from the apartment next door. This house is half the distance from my favourite wave, which softens the blow, and it means I can walk there if – or when – my car breaks down. Location. Location. Location.

Daisy is now in London and has just appeared in her first film, playing a glamorous chanteuse. She sings a cover of 'Anarchy in the UK' with Adam Ant, and 'Autumn Leaves' in French and English. I told her she'd thank me when she was trilingual!

275

We all just about fit in, until for reasons best known to my psychiatrist, I adopt a cute little puppy with huge paws who quickly grows to be a cute, gigantic puppy. Django weighs 60 kilos, he looks like a Doberman-Shetland pony cross and thinks he's a poodle. He has a habit of throwing himself into the lap of visitors that probably only I find irresistibly adorable.

Although the kids are teenagers it is still pretty full on looking after them while I continue to paint, organise shows and spend quality time with my surfboard. I get home at ten o'clock one night after a long day juggling my duties as taxi driver, cleaning lady, art star, fast food chef and basketball mum. Nat has been headhunted to join the squad in Ascain because he's almost 2 metres tall and that counts for a lot round here. I encourage him and then with typical overkill, I suggested he might get a basketball scholarship to an American university.

'I've only played twice Mum. I don't think I'll be joining the Harlem Globetrotters just yet!'

Ascain is a 30-minute drive inland and there's not a lot to do there of an evening. It's a picturesque Basque village in the foothills of the Pyrenees light on the nightlife, so I spend two nights a week hanging around in car parks. Tonight has been a particularly stressful session. After dropping him off, I walked halfway up a mountain with the dogs, just in case I wasn't tired enough already, and arrived back in the sports centre at dusk. I see an opportunity to get a bit of writing done, so I balance my notebook on the steering wheel, get out my pen and use the floodlights from the rugby pitch to see by. At that moment a whistle blows, a dog barks somewhere on the hillside and my monstrous puppy jumps out of the window and onto the pitch to join in the fun. It's the kind of incident that might be really, really funny in a family movie, but is really, really unfunny in real life. The only ones finding it less funny than myself are the 30 Basque rugby players on the pitch, but Django seems to find it bloody hilarious watching me chasing him in platform flip-flops and a frilly skirt under the bright lights.

I fluctuate between coaxing, 'Biccies! Come here, yummy meaty biccies,' and threats, 'I will have you fucking put down if you don't obey me. I'll take you back to the farm. I will sell you to a drug dealer.'

I finally win a tackle, bundle him into the car and repark in a dark corner hoping for Nat's sake that no one will know I'm his mother.

I still haven't recovered my cool when I get home. While I cook dinner I launch into my habitual whinge about my life of sacrifice.

'You have no idea how hard it is being a single mother. All I ever do is cook and clean and drive.' This is not strictly speaking true. The real reason I'm so exhausted is that I went for a surf with the Mamas during the short gap between school runs and basketball practice.

'Come on Mum, it's not like you go to *school*. How hard can it be?'

'You'll never understand how hard my life is until you have kids of your own.' I don't mention the surfing because I don't want to give them too much ammunition, but they may have already seen my wetsuit hanging up in the shower.

'Haha! Work?! All you ever do is surf and drink beer!'

'If only,' I sigh opening another Corona. 'I dedicate my whole life to you children. I'm a slave to your every whim.'

'Oh dear,' Alice laughs, 'what *will* you do when we're gone? Your life will be so empty. Oh, I know! You could get another dog. Why don't you get a husky and call it Alice, then you could rename the others Nat and Daisy, and you won't even notice we're gone.'

It's an amusing idea, but Alice is making the common error of misunderstanding Empty Nest Syndrome.

What do birds do when the fledglings spread their wings and disappear into the sunset? Do they sit around in the empty nest, watching daytime TV and crying into their sherry because the place seems so big and quiet all of a sudden?

Of course not. The birds realise that they no longer have to spend all day digging up their body weight in worms and regurgitating them into the mouths of their ungrateful chicks. They spread their own wings and go off to spend the summers in Iceland and winters in the tropics. Having spent the last 22 years digging up worms, I think that sounds like a really good idea.

'What will I do? Mmm, let me think. I know, I'll go on a surf trip round the world.'

'Oh.' Long silence. 'Can we come with you?'

SURF LIKE AN EGYPTIAN

The idea that I was ready to take on the great surf spots of the world may have been inspired by the Mamas surf rendezvous that morning.

I'm surfing a lot by myself now, but I join the Mamas whenever I can. It's always nice to hang out with the other women and get a bit of coaching and inspiration from Christophe and Johanna.

I hadn't meant to go today as I was overwhelmed by the To Do lists pinned to my walls. I am disorganised, verging on totally chaotic. I put it down to the overdevelopment of the creative right-hand side of my brain to the detriment of the left-hand side, which deals with organisation. I'm lost without lists. I'm the sort of person who will make a To Do list with 'Write list' at the top.

Alice looked over my shoulder the other day while I was making an essential list and burst out laughing.

'I can't believe you wrote that. You're such a bimbo!'

I look down and read what I've written: To Do – Not work.

I'm slightly annoyed and try to explain that this is the list of things that are *not* related to work, but probably are related to things she needs. But Alice has already replaced her earphones and left the room singing to a Katy Perry song.

I look down at my desk. Maybe Alice has picked up on something after all. You could certainly read it as 'Do not work'. Perhaps I should listen to the voice of my subconscious. Written on the lines below are: ring tax office, buy carpet shampoo, go to garage re bald tyres. Nothing too urgent. I can hear the swell from my bedroom and I know the Mamas are meeting soon. I remember the philosophy of surf: I can pay the taxes when it's flat.

The waves are perfect, if a little on the overhead, scary and generally fucking enormous side.

I try to persuade Christophe to take us down the coast to find something a little more relaxing, but driving away from the Perfect Wave and going to look for knee-high ladies' waves is too much to ask. I do some yogic breathing and try to get my big-wave hell woman head on as we walk across the beach. It's an Indian summer and the water is bright blue under a bright blue sky, sparkle factor is high and there are groups of surfers dotted about out to sea, bobbing around like a colony of sea lions, looking alarmingly small compared to the waves. Above them flocks of doves fill the air, swept down the valleys by the south wind.

Today's lesson is all about style and I recently realised how much of a stylist Christophe is. He was very encouraging when we started, congratulating us on every 'successful' wave, even if he had blinked and missed it.

But at a certain point our coach became more critical. One day during the summer, I came out of the water feeling like I'd taken the most unbelievable, miraculous, sublime wave. I walked up to the Bahia beach bar still shaking with excitement, expecting everyone to tell me how wonderful I am and hoping someone would buy me a beer.

Someone did buy me a beer, but not Christophe. His only comment, expressed less politely, was, 'You must get your turns more fluid.' Then he walked off.

'Did you hear that? I can't believe it. That was one of the best waves I've ever taken. Does he *remember* how long it took me to stand up?' I asked Johanna.

'Don't worry. It's a compliment. He must think you're getting good if it's worth criticising you.'

A couple of weeks later I went for a big wave. I took off and stood up for a split second before catapulting head first off the top of the wave, hitting the water with a thump, swirling round 'in the spin cycle', grabbing a breath when I could and then finally surfacing somewhere near Christophe, coughing and spluttering.

'Are you OK?'

'Hmm, yes I think so. Everything seems to be more or less in the right place.' I was waiting to hear what idiotic mistake I'd made this time.

'Well, *bravo*! I'm so pleased with you!' I looked around to see if he was talking to another Mama behind me.

'Why? I totally ate the dog bowl.' The French expression seemed to capture the disaster perfectly.

'Wilma, you went for the big one and you almost made it. Yes, I'm really proud of you.'

This will be one of the key points in my psychology of surf book: better to be ambitious and fail, than to compromise because, after all, it is only water.

Today we're learning that it's better to wipeout in style than to stay on the wave looking desperate. Christophe's a big muscly guy, but very graceful in the water, and I get the feeling that he would rather see us under the water than on top of it committing style errors. Number one on the style error list is sticking our bums out and waving our arms around as if we were doing ski exercises or sitting on an invisible toilet. He demonstrates this on the beach.

'Then, there's Wilma,' he laughs, 'who surfs like an Egyptian statue.' He imitates me surfing like a hieroglyph, straight legs, bent elbows and wrists, eyes half closed. I know it's not technically correct, but I think it looks quite cool. I might start wearing kohl and lapis lazuli eyeshadow.

I paddle out with my heart pounding and that old Bangles song 'Walk Like an Egyptian' stuck in my head. The girl band's bass and tambourine calm me down a bit.

I go way out and stay beyond the impact zone, for a while persuading myself that it really *is* better take a wave and fail than not to take a wave at all. When you've been out on the ocean long enough you get light-headed and feel possessed with the surf equivalent of flamenco dancers' duende. It may be something to do with forgetting breakfast and drinking too much coffee, it may be the hypnotic effect of the waves crashing onto the shore or an excess of negative ions in the salty haze over the water. It may be a desire to show off your new Egyptian surf moves to a bronzed demigod who's caught your eye.

I go for a wave, not looking back to see how big it is in case I come to my senses and panic. It's one of those days when everything seems to work. I cut across the face leaving a line of white water in my wake, do some turns that seem pretty fluid to me and ride the wave all the way in to the beach.

I go back out, and do it a few more times. The last one I share with Christophe. Sharing a wave should not to be confused with someone 'dropping in' on your wave, which provokes the surfing equivalent of road rage – wave rage – for similar reasons. Dropping in involves cutting you up and almost slicing you in two. It's pretty much like a driver pulling out in front of you at a roundabout, except the surfer is in the middle of a cosmic communion with the ocean so is full of righteous anger when the moment is cut short, tends to swear a lot and show his or her dark side. Sharing a wave is about sharing all that cosmic stuff, feeling full of peace and love, reverting to the inner hippy, and talking about good vibes and being stoked.

At one point I shout over to Christophe, *'Magnifique!'*

He probably thinks I'm talking about the waves or the beautiful view across the water, the golden light falling on the cliffs in Spain on the road to Santiago. He might even think I'm talking about the effortless cut-back he's carving across the water. But actually I'm talking about *my* last turn, which I think is one of my finest moments in surf, if not in my entire life.

We come out of the water and one of Christophe's other students is there looking a little green.

'That was beautiful, wasn't it? I mean it seemed a bit big at first, but it's really mellow. Oh, are you OK?' I ask, noticing his Pre-Raphaelite skin tone.

'God, I was *really scared* out there.'

The guy's a cool looking, twenty-something snowboarder from Toulouse, and I guess I assumed he could surf better than us having youth, attitude and tattoos on his side – maybe he did too. But he hasn't been surfing long and is suffering from post-traumatic surf syndrome, so I do 'the talk'.

'You know, next time you go out in small waves it'll seem easier, you just have to learn to enjoy the wipeout, it's only water.'

I look up and see the rest of the Surf Mamas come in together on a wave in a line, Waikiki style. I can't believe how good we've become; the Mamas solidarity has certainly paid off. I think back to the days when every wave was a wipeout, and every knee-high set seemed like a Hawaiian cloud break. When I dreamed of learning to surf, I honestly never thought I'd do this. I meant it when I said to Phil Grace that I wanted a board for 2-centimetre waves. I remember how Taryn and I wished deep down that it would be flat calm every week so we could just do the beer and bonding bit and skip the terrifying middle stage.

I feel so proud of us. I feel like telling the young guy, 'Don't worry, we were beginners too once. Now look at these awesome women!'

THE CRAIC

So the plan is in place – the Endless Summer trip round the world – every surfer's dream. You're footloose and fancy free, you sling a sarong and a bar of wax in your beach bag, grab your board and leave a note saying 'Gone Surfin'' on the table. Then you head off to wherever the best waves are breaking that week. You play Mary Poppins and tell your friends, 'I'll meet you in Bali when the wind shifts to the east.'

My nest is not yet empty, in fact there are times when it seems like it's splitting at the seams – like the time Django ate half the door. If I had looked carefully at our new nest I would have noticed that if there was space for another pet, it would have to be small one – a Russian hamster or, at a push, one of those handbag dogs popular with fashionistas that would tire after one circuit of a Chanel boutique. But I have a cuckoo in the nest, he won't stop eating and he won't stop growing. He opens the fridge and eats our food without bothering to remove the wrapping. He can demolish a chicken carcass in 30 seconds and he's chewed his way through the wicker sofa mistaking it for a chew toy.

Never mind, I can plan the surfari, and the first decision is where to start.

I've had an invitation to Nicaragua from the Silver Surfer who now spends winters on a piece of land he bought there above a deserted beach. But if we couldn't successfully rendezvous in a village with a couple of bars, we don't have much chance of meeting up in the Nicaraguan rainforest.

Australia is another option; an old friend from London has a cabana near Darwin. The fact that the surf is mediocre is academic as the water is infested with crocodiles, sharks and box jellyfish. The real attraction is the *après* surf – Ian is a travel writer who specialises in Aboriginal tourism and he has promised to take me to a body painting festival in Arnhem Land.

Following the birds to Iceland is another idea – cold water exotic. I'm slightly put off when I read in a blog by a Viking surfer that après-surf consists of stopping at a garage and pouring warm tap water over your head. I've spent more time than most in Icelandic garages, hitch-hiking being spectacular but slow. Surely there must be a break somewhere near a volcanic hot spring?

It's obvious where I should start, but I don't realise it until I see the cabbage.

I am engaged in what is described on my motivational chart as 'raising profile by use of social networking'. In theory making useful contacts, checking out galleries in New York, Los Angeles, Shanghai and Miami. In practice it means checking out what my friends – real and ethereal – are eating for breakfast round the world and inviting myself to stay on their sofas during my surfari. This is followed by posting up a few cute pictures of my puppy, checking the swell forecast and going for a surf. I'm just inviting myself to Trinidad to see someone I haven't seen for 30 years and had a crush on at college when I'm interrupted by the phone.

It's my ex-husband Nick ringing out of the blue to say he's on his way down from Paris, where he's been living for the last two years, and can I tell the children, who he hasn't seen for a while.

'That's nice. How long are you here for?'

He explains that things have taken a dramatic turn in the city, his girlfriend has changed the locks and he's in a service station outside Bordeaux with all his possessions in the back of a VW camper van.

'Oh wow!' he says as we talk, 'I just got out of the van, it's so warm down here. I love this heat – I think I'll move back to Olatua!' He always was impulsive.

I'm not sure that I'm quite ready for the reconstructed dysfunctional family. As I've mentioned several times, I live in a village with one main street, a couple of bars and a beach. If he moves back, my chances of bumping into him every time I go out for a litre of milk, a pint of beer or a wave are about 99 per cent.

'Oh that'll be nice for the kids,' I say as enthusiastically as possible. Although it also means he *can* look after them. This could be a good moment to start the world tour, leaving him to babysit. I calculate that it will take a couple of weeks for the novelty of childcare to wear off, so I should move quickly.

Just then I see the photo on Facebook – it's my friend Barbie from Baile na nGall, in the local bar with a giant cabbage, which has won a prize in the Dingle horticultural show.

Underneath the picture is written: Cabbages need a social life too. The craic at Begley's Bar.

Ah the craic, pronounced crack, but not to be confused with a class A drug. From the slang dictionary: 'Craic – Irish word for fun, enjoyment, partying, usually when mixed with alcohol and/or music.' And/or vegetables.

The photo makes me really want to go back to Ireland. I don't have a sudden craving for sauerkraut, but I do have a sudden craving for the craic in Begley's Bar.

That's it, of course, it's the perfect place to start my world tour – Baile na nGall – the place where I spent ten years as a Surf Widow!

By the time my ex arrives I've booked my ticket and Barbie has made up the spare bed.

GONE SURFIN'

Now I've decided where I'm going, I have to decide what to take.

I sling the wax, the sarong and the spare bikini in my bag, then I confront the first problem. How do you travel light with a 10-foot longboard?

I'm using this trip as trial run for the surfari and part of my plan had been to travel without maps, guidebooks and to rely on the kindness of strangers to lend me boards. I'd take pot luck with whatever was available: a kid's short board, an old door, a dugout canoe. I liked the element of chance and it seemed to fit with the carefree hippy ethos of a surf safari. But now I'm not so sure.

I weigh up the pros and cons of taking my board.

Pros: I will surf better on my own board.

Cons: The ticket for the board will cost more than my own ticket, and it will probably get damaged or even broken.

My board is really, really heavy, and I will arrive having not seen my friends for ten years stressing about dings, whinging about tendonitis and exhausted after a cross-country trek with a longboard under my arm.

I'm coming back through London, which will be an extra hassle and two more plane tickets.

If there's no surf I'll be pissed off that I brought it and then sink into the morose state I witnessed in those surf tourists who stopped at my house all those years ago.

The pros are on the light side, on the other hand I don't want to go back after all these years and fall on my arse in the mousse. I know this is really a trip about going home, about seeing my friends and reclaiming my past, but it is also the beginning of my world tour and a symbolic moment, so it would be nice to be able to stand up.

I can't even be sure of getting a wave – Irish waves are famous for being inconsistent, quixotic. Sometimes you'll get the lines of corduroy that announce the perfect swell, record-breaking waves over 20 metres high that have recently been surfed there or some huge but totally unsurfable swell that you have to leave for the dolphins and the killer whales. There's a chance you won't be able to stand up in the wind, let alone surf. Or you could get nothing at all. The weather forecast is not exactly comforting – 95 per cent chance of rain every day I'm there and what looks like a huge storm coming in.

I remember to stay Zen and not to behave like the morose surf bums I entertained back in my Surf Widow days. The only person who always caught a wave was The Gill, who lived ten minutes from the Swansea–Cork ferry. He would drop everything if he heard a promising shipping forecast, jump on an overnight crossing, arrive for breakfast, surf for a couple of days, and then go home with a live lobster in the cooler as a peace offering to his wife.

I'm in the Bar Basque with Phil Jarratt, my surf legend friend who is now based back in the land of Oz, but still jet-setting around the world in his laid-back way. Ireland is considered a pretty core destination and also has some of the biggest surfable waves in the world.

'Ireland – great. Someone just surfed a twenty-four-metre wave at Mullaghmore. Have you seen the video?'

I'm not sure if I want to. 'Not really what I have in mind.'

We move on from the subject of the record-breaking wave heights I'm going to surf and on to the problem of whether to take the board.

'Surf what you find there,' is Phil's advice.

'What if I can't surf it?'

'Then enjoy the wipeout and drink some Guinness.'

We are joined by an elegant French silver fox who enters in to the debate.

'I went to Easter Island last year. I didn't take my boards.'

We're slightly missing the point here that these guys *could* surf a short board, an old door or a dugout canoe while I couldn't.

But I decide they're right, I should leave it in the hands of fate. If this complete stranger went to Easter Island without a board, I don't need a board in Baile na nGall.

One thing I'm not going to borrow is a wetsuit. I know that you can do as many goddess workshops as you like, find enlightenment through yoga, empowerment through pole dancing, walk to the nose and hang ten, but you will never, ever feel like a goddess in a man's wetsuit that is three sizes too big. It will fill with water and you will look like the Michelin Man and feel like a walrus trying to surf.

On the other hand if you surf without a wetsuit in Ireland in October you will not feel anything: you will go instantly numb and be rushed to Tralee General Hospital with hypothermia. Although I have happy memories of the place as Alice was born there, this doesn't seem like a suitable ending for the first leg of the world tour.

Travelling light is easier when you're heading for the tropics than the Irish winter. After seeing the weather forecast I throw in every piece of neoprene in the house, mountain boots, fleeces, anoraks and ski socks by which time the bag is a bit on the heavy side.

By the time I've added a few bottles of wine, Bayonne chocolate and Espelette chillies, I can hardly lift it. Lucky I wasn't hoping to fit in a longboard as well.

I leave the fridge full of food, a list of instructions for my ex and a note saying 'Gone Surfin'' on the table.

RETURN TO TIR NA NÓG

My trip back to Ireland has acquired a homecoming quality, almost as if I had boarded a boat for the New World and couldn't return until I had a bag of gold nuggets to put behind the bar. I may not be Irish, but anyone who has spent ten winters in Baile na nGall has earned the right to a bit of sentimentality.

When we moved away, I promised my friends, my kids – and most importantly myself – that we'd be back every summer, but we haven't been back for ten years. The longer I left it the harder it got, the further away it seemed. I started dreaming that I was back and waking up half convinced I was. Eventually it seemed almost as if Baile na nGall only existed in the past. Perhaps I couldn't go back. Perhaps it's altered beyond recognition and I will find, like the warrior poet in the Oisín legend, the land has changed and my people have gone. There are rumours of a bowling alley where the old sheep market used to be and a new housing estate creeping up the mountainside.

Or maybe *I* have changed beyond recognition. I'll come across as a strange Frenchified surf chick, sit around in bars with my friends, fiddling with my beermat and eating pork scratchings in awkward silence as I realise we no longer know each other. Maybe I'll turn to dust when my feet touch Stradbally Strand – or worse still revert to my unfit earth mother persona and not know how to surf.

I fly into Dublin, which is nothing like coming home, because I don't know it at all, and my friend Kate is there to greet me. She shows no signs of not recognising the effortlessly chic French woman standing in front of her with a bag of wet neoprene and unbrushed hair.

'Hi honey, you have a bit of fishing net in your hair.'

We lighten the weight of my suitcase by drinking the wine and catching up with news of each other and our daughters, who used to play in the rock pools and go to parties together in chiffon fairy dresses, sequins and feathers. I'm glad to hear that Sibael, like my Daisy, is still going to parties in chiffon and sequins.

'Has it all changed?'

I've heard a lot of rumours about the changes in Ireland during years of the Celtic Tiger that transformed the country into an economic miracle before collapsing and leaving chaos in its wake.

'You'll see the ghost estates across the country, thousands of half built houses destined to be demolished before they were ever lived in.'

She describes the moment she knew the tiger wouldn't last. It was when she saw a €50 bottle of mineral water in her local supermarket, it was in a locked fridge and covered in Swarovski crystal.

'It's not even alcohol!' we laugh. I've just done a tour of Superquinn in Harold's Cross and I have to say it didn't look particularly bling.

'But, I think, in a way you'll find things are back to how they used to be.'

In the morning we say goodbye and she puts me on the train to my real destination, not Ireland, but the Kingdom of Kerry.

I settle down on the train and locate my mobile phone in a wetsuit boot. There's a text from Nat.

'Dad won't take me to basketball and there's no food in the house.'

The next five texts are along similar lines, but with a few more expletives in each version.

I reluctantly call home.

'What the hell Nat, I haven't even been gone twenty-four hours! What happened to the home-made lasagne I left in the fridge?'

'I ate it for breakfast.'

After some manic texting between Nat, Nick and myself, I establish that the kids are not starving and Ascain aren't about to lose their hoop man. I wonder if I should chuck the phone out of the window.

I sleep for a while and miss the abandoned suburbs and the dream houses called Tara, bulldozed to dust and gone with the wind.

I'm a bit alarmed when an over fifties bowling club join me in the carriage as we cross into the Kingdom. I'm worried that they're heading for the bowling alley in Dingle, which I see as a symbol of the unwanted change that might have transformed my former home.

I want romance and horses clattering up the streets, wellies in Dick Mack's and the wild, wild west: I don't want bowling teams from Dublin in Crimplene trouser suits.

Not that I have anything against bowling. Taryn and I often go on family bowling outings in Bayonne on winter afternoons when the weather is atrocious and the kids can't be persuaded to surf.

I get in conversation with the woman sitting next to me, who is walking with a frame.

'I'm not bowling, dear,' she says. 'I'm just going for the craic.'

'Where exactly are you going?' I ask nervously.

'Killarney. How about you?'

I tell her.

'And why are you going to Dingle dear?'

I think about it. To see my long lost friends, to rediscover my past and the most beautiful place on earth. To prove something to myself, that I have changed, that I can surf the waves I watched from the beach when I was an earth mother. And to start my surf tour of the world.

'I'm just going for the craic, too.' This seems to sum it up.

The final leg of the journey is on the last bus from Tralee. By this time I'm pretty glad not to have a surfboard under my arm. I wait impatiently in the bus stop drinking tepid tea and eating scones, remembering my first trip along the peninsula: the wild fuchsia hedges, the red-haired boy in a donkey cart laden with carrots, the pod of wild dolphins in the surf at

Inch. I fell in love with Ireland that day and often think if it had been raining my life would have taken a very different turn.

The bus leaves at sunset and the hedges are still made of fuchsia, caught in the setting sun like an over saturated technicolour movie. I could easily believe that I'm in one of my lucid dreams and not here at all, looking out at the brightly painted houses with gardens full of arum lilies and unnaturally blue hydrangeas, the Slieve Mish Mountains and behind them the legendary throne of Finn McCool covered in purple heather.

The new estate is not as bad as I imagined. As a Londoner I couldn't help but imagine it rising up from the peat bog like a Tower Hamlets council block complete with graffiti, drug dealers and lifts stinking of urine. So the kitsch row of fake thatched cottages sprawling on the outskirts of town is almost a pleasant surprise.

Barbie is waiting for me at the fishing port. She's an artist, her images a mix of Celtic, African and Navajo tribal patterns spread from her canvases onto her furniture, crockery and her clothes. She's waiting for me in a jacket covered in Aboriginal-inspired fish and bird motifs – no question of not recognising each other. There's a food and drink festival in progress and the town is packed, so first stop is Cúl Gairdín, Barbie's holistic vegetarian restaurant that doubles as art gallery. We have a bowl of vegetable soup, which probably doesn't actually have the prize-winning cabbage in it, but it seems symbolic and tastes delicious.

We decide to grab a beer before heading over the hill. The 52 bars are crammed with bearded men in a scruffy tweed jackets, typical Dingle natives who could be musicians, potters, sheep farmers, fishermen, healers, poets or film directors, all drawn to Main Street by the power of the Dingle ley line. I'm glad to see there are still knitted sheep in the window of the wool shops, they're still selling wellies in Dick Mack's, bicycles and coal in Foxy John Moriarty's and duck food in Currans. It's reassuring although I have no ducks, I've lost my fireplace and the wellies wouldn't fit in my bag along with all the neoprene, and of course they all still sell Guinness.

Barbie lives on the mountainside above Baile na nGall with her husband Pat and charming 14-year-old son Eoghan, her other son Robert, is a musician in Dingle. She has warned me that there are houses all around her now and that I won't know the place.

When we arrive I realise that it's a joke – there are three times as many houses as when I left, but it's still only three houses. One belongs to my friend Helena, and when she comes down from the mountain riding bareback on her horse with a bunch of montbresia lilies in her hand, I know that my people are still my people and the land has not changed beyond recognition.

Pat is one of the Baile na nGall fishermen. Since salmon fishing was banned, his boat has become an angling boat taking tourists and locals out beyond the Blaskets to catch fish or to look at the dolphins, seals, whales and sharks.

Sharks? I thought one of the perks of cold-water surf was no sharks to worry about. I know they're not meant to attack in cold water but I double check.

'Don't worry, they're only blue sharks, nurse sharks, bull huss, basking sharks.'

I know basking sharks eat plankton, but having seen them on the pier at Baile na nGall they look kind of big and toothy.

'And you're sure they don't attack humans, even with global warming?'

'Nah. I'd be more worried about killer whales if I was out there.'

He's joking, I think, and I decide not to worry about a killer whale mistaking me for a seal, a basking shark mistaking me for a bit of plankton or a humpback breaching and landing on me.

THE MARY CELESTE

The following day Barbie and Pat have to go to a wake in the next village. The water's glassy calm, and I don't yet have a board or any transport – although Helena did offer to lend me a horse – so surfing is out, and I go for a long walk round Smerwick Harbour.

Barbie and Pat drop me near the graveyard and I walk for hours to the fort at Dún an Óir where the English army massacred hundreds of Spanish and Italian soldiers during a rebellion. I keep going across the 'black beach' where tales are told of human bones and Armada gold buried in the sand. I cross the river to Murreigh beach where they used to hold horse races at low tide in the summer, and where the kids and I stood in the dunes cheering Helena on in her horse-drawn sulkie cart.

I remember the day I went fishing with Nick and he pulled up a bull huss – a catshark – in the net. It was almost as big as the 3-metre rubber dinghy we were in. The huss was tangled in the net and getting angry, and Nick asked me to get a knife and to help cut it free. I sat there screaming my head off until he'd finished the job. I don't think I ever went fishing with him again. I don't think he ever asked me. After that I stayed on dry land making the mayonnaise.

I always remember Nick saying as I mixed a strong Kerry margarita to get over the shock, 'Come on Wilma, it was only a bull huss!' Like I didn't deserve a drink after being in a rubber dinghy with a catshark!

Apart from a farmer I pass in a lane I'm alone all day, walking all the time towards Mount Brandon, a shroud of mist blowing down the slopes like a waterfall, a light drizzle falling, the sort of soft day that is 'good for your complexion'.

Although I seem to be wandering aimlessly, I know where I'm heading – back to my house. After a couple of hours I'm at the bottom of the dirt road wondering if I can walk back in to the past down a fuchsia-fringed lane with grass growing up the middle.

I get a shock when I see the house. Nothing has changed. The flower pots haven't been moved, the salvaged driftwood and junk furniture on the patio is just as we left it, the dry stone barbecue I built in the corner. The pampas grass has taken over the rose bed, the cordyline palm is 6-metres high and my honeysuckle is growing over the door. The vegetable patch is overgrown – the only survivor is an obscure Mexican herb called epazote, which at some point seemed a vital ingredient of my life. I squeeze through the gate and look through the window.

Everything is exactly as we left it: the Mexican tiles round the fireplace, pale turquoise walls and lemon wood panelling. The owners have even bought the exact same Matisse print we had and hung it over the mantelpiece. If this was an art house movie, I would see myself sitting in front of the Mexican tiled fireplace writing out a salsa recipe and realise I was caught in some weird time warp.

And there's a For Sale sign stuck in the hedge! I go back later with Helena, who has asked the estate agent to show us round.

Stranger and stranger, the bed is in the same place and on the table beside it is the book I was meaning to read when we left – *The Girl at the Lion d'Or*. But most bizarre is the studio. The halogen lights haven't moved: they're still at the same angle, covered in cobwebs, focused on the back wall where I used to paint. There are still paint stains where my canvases hung, although the paintings are now hanging in London and Paris and Biarritz. There are splats of oil paint and kid's poster paint on the floor, I recognise the colours from when they body painted each other.

Above the dining room table is the drawing my friend Sophie Parkin gave me for my fortieth birthday. I'd been upset when I lost it; it must have been in the attic.

'Er that's mine actually,' I start to say, fully intending to take it off the wall.

'Do you think I can take it?' I whisper to Helena.

She's not sure. Maybe I'll just leave it there and buy back the house.

It's like the Mary Celeste, the ship found sailing in the Atlantic, abandoned but untouched – dinner laid on the galley table and tea still warm in the teapot, according to nineteenth-century mariner's legend.

I have a feeling that if I opened the freezer it would be full of Ziploc bags of seaweed and my home-made lasagne.

'I don't want to sound weird,' I say, 'but I feel like it's destiny that I should have my house back.'

'You should.'

'Not weird at all,' agrees the estate agent. 'It's destiny.' Of course he'd be getting a percentage and I haven't got the money in my pocket or anywhere else, but it does seem like a sign and a half.

STRADBALLY

Luckily I don't have to surf a plank of wood or an old door after all. My first offer of a board is from Finn McCool – or to be more precise, Ben Farr from Finn McCool's surf shop. It's an old foam beginner's board, and I'm worried that it will feel like day one at surf school and that I'll revert and surf like a beginner. On the other hand, foam boards float well so even if I don't return triumphant I am quite likely to return.

But I'm very happy when my friend Paul offers me a wooden longboard.

Paul McCarthy was one of the only other surfers when we lived here. He was a teenager going on voyages of discovery with Nick, looking for unsurfed waves in freezing Irish winters.

I go to Tralee to hire a car and then meet him in one of the famous music bars in Dingle to collect the board. The room falls silent as a woman with a beautifully pure voice sings a song I remember Daisy playing on the tin whistle:

'Oh please ne'er forget me though waves now lie o'er me
I was once young and pretty and my spirit ran free.'

It's the sort of melancholy Irish music that fills you with an aching nostalgia for the green fields of home, your family and a sweetheart. I feel quite carried away by emotion, but pull myself together realising I don't have to swim over the deepest ocean to see my loved ones again. I'm not on a prison ship to Australia, I'm actually here in Kerry in a nice warm bar with a pint of Guinness. I get back to the subject of surf.

I last saw Paul in Olatua, en route from Morocco in a camper van. He left a couple of carpets from the kasbah that I had on the floor of the house for years.

After that, he tells me, he travelled around South America working with Land Rover off-road rallies, and with the money from that he built a house – by which he means literally built it brick by brick – got married and had three children. So Paul's back more or less where he was when we left. The board is a beautiful wooden 10-foot longboard from Ecuador and it's perfect for me. Not only easy to catch waves with, but extremely classy and stylish.

Next morning I strap it to the roof of the hire car and set off over the pass to see whether the most beautiful place on earth still deserves its title. I have to stop several times on the pass, partly to take photos, partly because I feel my breath taken away by the beauty of the landscape. I stop at the top and look down across Brandon Bay, half covered in cloud with shafts of sunlight breaking through and hitting the water, lighting it up like a sheet of silver. I don't come down a born-again anything, but I can understand why people believe in God or leprechauns or the pot of gold at the end of the rainbow. You would have to be a hard-hearted atheist not to feel spiritual as you cross the Conor Pass on a day like this.

My main worry today is not whether I'll have to surf 24-metre waves, but whether I'll be able to find a wave at all: Stradbally Strand seems like my best shot.

After talking to the girls last night I'm guessing that one thing I *don't* have to worry about is crowds.

'There must have been a contest or something last weekend. I've never seen so many people in the water!'

'How many?' I ask.

'We counted twelve.'

After paddling out into 120 people a few weeks ago it's a bit ironic to be scouring the sea for other surfers, but going out all alone is not generally a good idea just in case you hit your head and get carried off in current or something. Not only do I not see any other surfers, I don't see anyone at all.

This side of the peninsula is even wilder and less built up. I drive through villages and fields of bright green grass seeing no living thing apart from a couple of cows. I stop at Stradbally and walk onto the beach and my feet touch the sand without any drama except that I remember my first night in Ireland, camped right here in the dunes in a tiny tent with my husband and baby Daisy.

After my first six months of sleep deprivation I was a little tired to say the least. I lay on my sleeping bag in the sand, looking out over the beach in the hazy sunshine on a Sunday afternoon. A few families had brought picnics, and farmers walked on the beach in Sunday suits or sat in fold-out chairs reading the papers. As I watched a man came and raced his greyhounds along the beach. Next a couple of people galloped past bareback on horses, then a rusting home-made beach buggy passed by like something out of *Mad Max*. Finally a white van came speeding across the stony beach, pulling a young guy on skis who was whooping and screaming with excitement.

'This place is completely crazy,' I said to my husband. 'Let's come and live here.'

We left London three months later.

The waves could be classed as even too small for the Mamas so I drive on until I reach the end of the road at the far end of the bay where a small wave or a large ripple is forming over a sand bank. Travellers' lore is that wherever you get the most deserted, most unspoiled, most beautiful beaches on earth, a German camper van will have got there before you. German travellers seem to have a homing instinct for these places that can be annoying, but in this instance I'm very pleased to see the camper van because in all my excitement I have forgotten the board wax. There's a wreath of plastic hibiscus flowers hanging over the rear view mirror so I know I'm in luck. The traveller looks a bit like a hobbit and speaks no English. The only German I can remember is, '*Weissbier und Sauerkraut mit Kartoffelsalat, bitte.*' Beer and cabbage with potato salad, please. I'll save that line for later when I come out of the water, and do a board-waxing mime to avoid saying, 'Sex Wax, *bitte*' as I am half dressed.

If I do get swept away by a freak wave or hit by a passing humpback, this guy can throw out the insubstantial plastic ring I saw tied to a rope in the dunes and save me.

I could tell a fisherman's story at this point as there were no witnesses to my first surf in Tir na nÓg, but I can honestly say my main fear is tripping in the seaweed as I surf ankle-high waves in knee-deep water – or knee-high waves in ankle-deep water. But as far as atmosphere goes you can't really beat this place: the clouds towering above the mountain, the curve of the empty beach, the white sand. I'm proud of myself for actually managing to surf something so small. The hobbit is honking his horn when anything that could be classed as a wave appears on the horizon. In the surf world this evocative sound herald's a warning *not* to get caught under a big set; here, it's telling me that a wave, almost too small to see, is on the way.

I try a few cross steps to amuse him because the wooden board seems made for it.

The cross step move is a way of getting elegantly to the nose of the board by crossing your feet, which will earn you lots of points in a longboard competition and kudos in the water once you master it. In my case it seems more like a good way of tripping over my feet and falling off a nice wave, so I go back to a less elegant but equally effective move I call 'the shuffle'.

I get about 20 tiny waves before the tide comes up and they stop breaking. The big advantage of surfing alone is you get all the waves.

I'm pleased with the first surf, the waves may not have been spectacular, but the scenery made up for it. I stop in Castlegregory for a traditional Irish lunch, a packet of Tayto crisps, a bottle of red lemonade and a Tiffin bar from the village shop.

Helena tells me later that if I'd turned the corner I would have found a big new supermarket that has an organic salad bar specially for surfers, but I'm somehow glad I didn't. I liked the corner shop with duck food, flowery aprons, dusty postcards of kittens that had probably been there since last time I stopped by, Tunnock's tea cakes and plastic-wrapped Kilmeadan 'the fillet of Cheddar'.

On the way home I stop at Finn McCool's for a cup of tea and a chat with Ben. I buy some wax, just in case I do reach a deserted beach without its friendly German traveller, and a sweatshirt saying, 'Europe's most Westerly Surf Shop' as a trophy. It's considered cool among hard-core surfie travellers to wear faded T-shirts from exotic locations – the painless version of the sailor's tattoo from far-flung lands. It's a bit too cool though and Alice steals it when I get home.

'But you don't surf!'

She pulls rank. 'I was born in Tralee.'

SURF WIDOW TO SURF MAMA

There are a lot of hi tech ways you can predict the swell these days: Internet sites, iPhone apps and live webcams on the beach if you don't want to run the risk of going to a beach and finding that the wind is onshore.

This is all great and I'm a big fan of technology, but it's a little geeky and not nearly as much fun as the old fashioned way – going to the bar in Baile na nGall for a pint of Guinness and asking the fishermen.

I'm relieved to see that Tigh TP bar hasn't turned into a theme pub or a bowling alley in my absence: the green and gold Kerry Gaelic football flag hangs over the fireplace; assorted number plates from round the world are nailed up on the walls between whiskey bottles; Sean B is behind the bar, handsome as ever; and his boat is still on the slip outside.

Barbie and Pat haven't told anyone I'm coming, so I'm greeted with a suitable level of surprise when I walk into the bar not having seen anyone for ten years. I feel as if I *had* been in the New World and come back with a bag of gold nuggets.

Strangely enough, despite the surprise that I'm here, no one seems in the least surprised that I'm here on a surf trip. Perhaps they saw my potential as an extreme sports hero before I did, as I sat on the beach in my bikini through storms and torrential rain for all those years, swimming every New Year's Day whatever the weather was chucking at me.

The forecast on the other hand is slightly alarming.

'Going up to four metres by the end of the week,' is not what I wanted to hear.

'Blimey can it really *be* four metres?' It's a very stupid question, but I have just come back from surfing the smallest waves ever surfed in Brandon Bay.

'It can be a lot more,' Pat laughs, thinking I must have a pretty bad memory. I remember watching spray 15-metres high in Clogher; the day the car almost blew off the cliff; the day we got down to a beach covered in 2-metres of foam, not pollution, just foam whipped up by the storm; the day the roof blew off; the day the rusty trawler smashed against the rocks at Slea Head; and the 24-metre waves surfed at Mullaghmore.

I maybe a big-wave hell woman who surfs fucking enormous waves without even smudging her mascara, but I'm not mad.

The general consensus is that if I want to surf on the westernmost beach where I first had the revelation that I wanted to be a surfer, I'd better do it tomorrow morning. And if I'm going to do that – still considered fairly bonkers by fishermen – I'd better have another pint to set me up with B vitamins and iron and 'the eating in the drinking of it'.

There are two bars in Baile na nGall, one either side of the pier, and it's considered impolite to go to one and not the other, so we head over to Begley's for another shipping forecast and another pint. By the time we head back up the hill I've recruited Barbie and Helena for the Baile na nGall chapter of the Mamas along with most of the other women in the village and decided that I'm buying my old house back.

So here I finally am, back on the westernmost beach in Europe, just along from the westernmost bar, underneath the westernmost beehive hut. It's still as wild and windswept and unspoilt as it was before, with the green, green fields falling into the ocean, the sheep and the arum lilies, and the gannets wheeling overhead. Barbie has taken my place as the westernmost beach bunny in Europe, suitably dressed in a skirt covered in Celtic crosses and Hawaiian vegetation, and I am nervously pulling on a damp wetsuit with the longboard from the Ecuadorian jungle at my feet. Paul arrives with his two-year-old son, Ozzie, who is off school sick. I was hoping Paul would come out with me, but the babysitter is sick too.

Predictably there is no one on the beach, but someone has been here and drawn a huge heart in the sand that seems like a good omen. I have given up on the idea of stumbling across other surfers by chance, but I try to persuade Paul to come in with me and leave Ozzie on the beach with Barbie.

'Should I go out alone?' I ask Paul.

'Sure you'll be grand, it's really mellow. Listen, I'd put my kids in that.'

You should never let this kind of comment lull you into a false sense of security – I've seen kids following their dads up the beach screaming and crying, including my own. But I see one last chance for a bit of company.

'Ozzie, do you want to come surfing with Auntie Wilma?'

Ozzie's face crumples in alarm wondering who this crazy woman is. I used to be so good with kids before I took up surfing.

When the moment comes the choice is paddle out alone or not at all. I set off with a slight flutter in my chest, and like St Brendan I am wondering if I am about to paddle off the edge of a flat earth. Or maybe the *Wizard of Oz* moment will be reversed and I'll dive under a wave and come out to a world of black and white, revert to a pre-Surf Mama self, my fear of waves will come flooding back just like the big cold shore break I am about to wade through.

Then I'm out there alone in the ocean, which appears dark from above, but as I dive into the waves the light shines through the water turning it emerald green and crystal clear. When I plunge through the foam it's like bathing in champagne.

My journey back to the westernmost beach has definitely been worth it, and as I sit alone in the ocean I realise that it doesn't even matter if I don't get a wave, I'm here.

I once thought that if I learned to surf, everything else would fall into place. I'm not sure if it has or if none of the rest matters anymore now that I can surf.

I look out towards the Blaskets imagining the underwater cliffs, the kelp forests and wrecks of pirate ships, the lost treasure of the Armada sunk to the ocean bed crawling with starfish, the whales and sharks, the other side of the islands, then 'next parish Manhattan'.

Looking towards the shore there's the whitewashed crucifix on the road above, with Mount Eagle rising up behind. Beyond that is Mount Brandon, the lanes where I picked blackberries for crumble with my children, the school where they learned to read and write in Irish, and the village hall where Daisy first took to the stage in Irish dancing contests and always came back fuming because she got the 'loser's medal'. My house, the studio with the paint marks on the wall, the vegetable patch where I tried to grow chillies one waterlogged Irish summer and the bars where the old farmers waltzed on Sunday nights.

I see a lump of dark water coming towards me, as it hollows out and starts to break I paddle and the elegant wooden board from the other side of the ocean takes off. When I stand up Barbie and Paul cheer as I surf towards the beach. The seaweed on the rocks will have to wait for another earth mother to come and harvest it. On the sand, visible only to me, is the faintest imprint of the beach blanket where I once sat eating home-made banana loaf with my children and wondered if I was too old and too scared to ever learn to surf.

I think about the journey that has brought me full circle, back to this place where I had the revelation that I wanted to be a surfer all those years ago. It seems like such a short distance from the beach into the ocean, only a couple of hundred metres.

It's funny to think of everything I've gone through to get onto this wave – all the wipeouts and bruises and feelings of inadequacy, but also all those terrifying and hilarious Saturday afternoons with the Mamas Surf Club that have finally paid off. But it wasn't really about doing a press-up or even standing up on a surfboard, it was about proving that I wasn't too old or too scared to do this, that I could transform myself from Surf Widow to Surf Mama.

ABOUT THE AUTHOR

Wilma Johnson is an artist and writer born in London in 1960. She has a degree in Fine Art from St Martin's College of Art. During the 1980s she found inspiration for her paintings while hitch-hiking round Iceland and Lapland, Italy and the Scottish Highlands. In 1987 she spent a year travelling round Mexico and Guatemala, following the fiesta and painting in rundown hotel rooms.

In 1991 she moved to a fishing village on the Dingle Peninsula in Ireland, where she lived for ten years, before moving to Biarritz in 2001 to become a surfer. She has three children and way too many animals.

www.surfmama.me

THE

Ribbons

ARE FOR

Fearlessness

a journey

CATRINA DAVIES

THE RIBBONS ARE FOR FEARLESSNESS

A Journey

Catrina Davies

ISBN: 978 1 84953 447 5   Paperback   £8.99

... fearlessness has got nothing to do with being unafraid. It's about doing things anyway, getting on with it, living, whether you're afraid or not... Courage is about being who you are with your whole heart.

Fuzzy-haired, neurotic, cello-playing Catrina is devastated when her lover, Jack, leaves her to go surfing on the other side of the world. Trapped in a dead-end job and torn by his departure, Catrina dreams of running away. But how do you run away when you're flat broke? Luckily, her friend Andrew comes up with a plan: they'll get an old van, turn it into a camper and busk their way from Norway to Portugal, via the midnight sun.

When Andrew is killed in a tragic accident Catrina decides to go it alone, with disastrous consequences, until her experiences on the road gradually teach her the real meaning of love, courage and above all else, the importance of following her dreams.

This is an unforgettable story of a journey like no other – a deeply emotional and inspirational debut by a unique storyteller.

Catrina Davies is based in Cornwall, where she surfs and plays the cello. She has performed at numerous festivals, including Glastonbury, and is recording her debut album.

Have you enjoyed this book?
If so, why not write a review on your favourite website?

If you're interested in finding out more about our books, find
us on Facebook at **Summersdale Publishers** and follow us on
Twitter at **@Summersdale**.

Thanks very much for buying this Summersdale book.

www.summersdale.com